The
BIBLE
Of
Bible Questions

To Mr and Mrs. TUNSTALL,
God Bless your family.
He That FINDETH a WIFE...
FINDETH A GOOD Thing AND
OBTAINETH FAVOR OF The Lord.
ENJOY!!!

Shelton Roseboro

GOD Bless

Shelton Rose 5/2/2020

P.S. SEE PAGE # 12

:)

ISBN 978-1-64028-264-3 (paperback)
ISBN 978-1-64028-265-0 (digital)

Christian Faith Publishing, Inc.
832 Park Avenue
Meadville, PA 16335
www.christianfaithpublishing.com

The Library of Congress certificate of Copyright registration information already obtained on effective date, August 03, 2015. Registration Number TXu 1-978-091 per Maria A. Pallante, United States Register of Copyrights and Director.

All scriptures are from the King James Version of the Holy Bible.

Cover design by Anthony Wingfield II. To contact, send emails to: eighty9design@gmail.com

Printed in the United States of America

Contents

PAUL'S EPISTLES TO THE CHURCHES

PAUL'S EPISTLES TO FRIENDS

GENERAL EPISTLES

APOCALYPTIC

CATEGORIZED GOSPEL QUESTIONS

Foreword

Have you considered the state this world would be in if no questions had ever been asked or answered? Without questions, and corresponding answers, how colorless and uninformed our lives would be. The English Oxford Dictionary defines a question as, a sentence worded or expressed to elicit information. Such received knowledge has the ability to inform and shed light, reveal truth and debunk error, give understanding or direct and change one's course and beliefs.

The Bible of Bible Questions has been ultimately compiled to show God's love and tender care. It was God's love that sought Adam in the Garden of Eden when God asked Adam "Where art Thou"? In the Garden of Gethsemane, Jesus asked Peter, "What, could ye not watch [pray] with me one hour"? Jesus' desire was not to shame Peter, but because of His love, to cause Peter to understand the help and protection that can be received through prayer. Likewise, the Apostle Paul asked certain disciples "Have ye received the Holy Ghost since ye believed?" Paul didn't view them as "lesser Christians," for his desire was that they could experience and know the love and power of God that would eventually be shed abroad in their hearts and poured out on them by this same Holy Ghost. God is love and His love is reflected in every word He has ever spoken, whether in the form of questions or not.

In *The Bible Of Bible Questions*, Shelton Roseboro has carefully compiled and captured the essence of both The Old and New Testament canon in a unique and inquisitive platform that challenges each student of God's Word to continue to search the scriptures, for in them is life.

Enjoy the journey!

Jennifer J. Nicholson
Rhema Christian Center Church, Wash. DC

Numerical Breakdowns*

By The Numbers:

Number of Questions in the Bible-3,340
Number of Questions, Old Testament-2,343
Number of Questions, New Testament-997

Number of Questions Jesus Asked-323**

The Gospel According to Matthew-100
The Gospel According to Mark-69
The Gospel According to Luke-101
The Gospel According to John-53

Number of Questions Asked of Jesus-144

The Gospel According to Matthew-35
The Gospel According to Mark-29
The Gospel According to Luke-30
The Gospel According to John-50

Number of Questions Asked Neither By Nor to Jesus-152

The Gospel According to Matthew-38
The Gospel According to Mark-20
The Gospel According to Luke-32
The Gospel According to John-62

Questions? Or Not!-54
Old Testament-43
New Testament-11

*The numbers that appear are approximates, due to the fact that some questions in the Bible appear to end with exclamation points, to the which, have also been recorded and included in the totals.

**Jesus; while making a point telling parables, mention various characters in such parables, that not only voiced particular concerns, but also posed various questions, to the which, have been recorded as originating from and belonging to, Jesus himself.

***The total number of questions ascribed to Jesus are not exclusive or independent of the pattern of the synoptic gospels themselves, which include similar stories recorded by the writers to whom each gospel book is attributed; so the same question is recorded in the totals, the exact number of times that same question appears throughout; even throughout the whole Bible.

Acknowledgements*

1) To God The Father, Jesus The Son, and The Holy Spirit: thank you for the power and the vision to receive Jesus as Lord and this book to His glory.

2) To my earthly and late father, Leandrow Roseboro Sr. for his love and ever tender spirit.

3) To my Mother, Willie Mae Peterson-"Evangelist Mommy". Thank you for your undying love and support, and life, even before we knew that we could live it more abundantly.

4) To the late Bishop Clarence C. Givens, the founder and Sr. Pastor of the Rhema Christian Center Church of N.E. Washington D.C., who taught me via God's word that it is alright to love God and to desire and apprehend God's best.

5) To the Late Bishop Lewis T. Tait Sr. Pastor of Faith Bible Church, of N.E. Washington. DC., and Mother Christine Tait, for teaching me that "People don't care about how much you know, until they know, how much you care". Thanks Bishop.

6) To my dear twin brother Sherwood "Mickey" (and his wife Mitzi Roseboro), and to my brother Wayman and sisters Celestine, Diane and Lavora; I wouldn't trade you guys for the world; and to both; my late brother Leon and sister Gwendolyn "Shang", we miss them both.

7) To the late Clea Arthur ("PaPa") Nicholson, who was a man truly called by God.

8) To Jennifer Nicholson and her family members Doug, Jackie Hartsfield, Leroy Hartsfield, Fay, Shronda, Uncle James, Raymond, Dennis, Jessica, Juan, and Jesse, for their untiring love and support.

9) To my Pastors Arvel and Brenda Givens for fighting the good fight and keeping their faith in Christ concerning me.

10) To the late Rhema Christian Center Church's Minister of Music, Anthony M. "Tony" Jefferson, Sr., who taught me that "It's not

who's right, it's what's right", and to his beautiful wife sister Donna Jefferson, and to their children, as well as to Claude "Jeff" and Margie Jefferson.

11) To the late Mr. Frank DeMaio, my High School guidance counselor, basketball coach, father figure, and friend, who "made" me take Creative Writing instead of Home Economics in the tenth grade, and to his lovely wife Mrs. DeMaio, and their daughter, Denise DeMaio Davis and family.

12) To Minister James and Evangelist Dorothy Brown (Forever encouraging and supportive).

13) To Doris (Roseborough) Wright for her long time love of the Lord and friendship; and to her husband Franklyn.

14) To Adrena Brown, who God used to tell me that the four hundred and sixty questions that I had already collected at the time, was actually a book.

15) To Bilyana Lilly, who is an distinguished author in her own right, who extended me the proposal that she submitted for her own book entitled *"Russian Foreign Policy Toward Missile Defense: Actors, Motivations, and Influence"* as a guide; and to her humble husband Sale Lilly (thanks for giving it "The Old college try").

16) To Anil Kochukudy who brought order to the chaos of a manuscript that I presented to him. Thanks again Anil.

17) I would be remiss if I didn't thank Christian Faith Publishing for availing themselves to aspiring authors like myself. Thank you, editors, typesetters, illustrators, cover folk, finance team, and a special thanks to Adam Mellott, my Publications Specialist. You guys rock.

18) Thanks also to; The Mighty Men of Valor from La Casa Transitional Rehabilitation Program (NW Washington DC), Pastor Dr. Everett W. Jenkins and the Gethsemane Missionary Baptist Church Ministers and Family (Bunn N.C.), Dave Riggs, William "Billy" Sussman, Andy Spano, Lonnie, Vivian, Michael and Richard Stafford, Kenny, David and Phillip Ford, Garrett and Derek Pastures, Brother Melville Shields, Mickey Oliver, Gilbert Harris, Allen and Greg Fisher, Phyllis Fisher, Pat and Teddy Kennedy, Randy Carpenter, Joe Gibson, Pastor Vincent Wiggins, Pastor Tony Hart, Mr. Runston Louis, Mr. Wasserman, Elder John Godwin, Paul Yizer, Glenn Weinstein, Melissa Toll, MaryAnn DePaulo, Lisa Schuchman, The Dobbs Ferry Cheerleaders, Stuart Sarnoff esq., Richard Delmerico, Patrick Ricci, the late Joey Yarabeck, Ricky

Miano, Sandy Youmans, Debbie Schapira, RoRo Annicchiarico, Russell Rosenberg, Coach Warzycki, Mr. Morgenstern, Scott Hall, Julio Berrios, Mia Baker, Ronald Watson, Reggie Harris, Arrington Ward, Vondell McKinley and family, My Library of Congress family, Shirley Berry (Because of the tracks you kept on your desk, I was found of Christ), Gospel Rescue Ministries, Minister Don Melvin, the late Mitch Snyder, the Center for Creative Non-Violence (CCNV),Lambro Papadopoulos, the late Minister Reggie Brogsdale, Greg Payne, Stephen Miller, Mr. Leslie Jones, Mr. Stewart, Benny Lake, Morris Crute, Michael Lyndon, Bernard Toone, Walt Brickowski, George Tino, Coach William "Hawkshaw" Wallace, Dwayne Lyons, Coach "Cos", Graham Home for Children (thanks for rescuing me), Dobbs Ferry High School and Middle School (thanks for teaching me), Miss Hodgins, Ms. Rose, Sheldon Liftin, Coach "Wild Bill" Kohl, Mr. Hildenbrand, Mr. Presley, Pastor (Elder) Louis T. Tait Jr, Lisa and Essence Tait. and the Faith Bible Church family, the late Mother Evangelist Barbara Best, Lois Tillery, Missionary Sylvia Wayman, "Bucky" Tillery, Minister Michael Cola, Deacon Jones, Sister Martha Johnson, Deacon Danny White, Elder Robert and Sister Linda McCurdy, Elder John and Sister Jackie Yates, Deacon Emmett and Paula Wade, Deacon Vincent Washington and family, Minister Eudora and Deacon Archie Heath, Deacon Trevor and Sister Cynthia Campbell, Sister Cora Thorne, Elder John Maddox, Pastor Barbara Belton, Bishop Stephen and Pastor Nya Ann Small, Ministers Greg and Chanda Adams, Sister Christal Alston and Sister Zondra Miller, Sister Deloris Hunter, Missionary Ella Flowers, Sister Marva Parker, Sister Ethel Kennedy, Sister Ethel M. Smith, Deacon George Stokes Jr., and Sister Katrina Stokes, Pastor George Stokes III, Minister Santesia Jones, Minister Georgia Crawford, Gregory Pippins, Brother John Austin, BettDarling, Pastor Denise and Minister Paul McDowell, Katie Miller, Sister Lynette Nurse, Minister Vaughn and Sister Kerrie McDowell, Juan and Moses Coulter, Evangelist David and Sister Cheryl Harrington and sons, Deacon Aaron and Sisters Janice, Casey and Blair Cooper, Elder Martin and Sister Denise Johnson, Sister Crystal Blair, Sister Cassandra Payne, Sister Agnes Brooks, Brother Mike and Sister Monica Hawkins, Barbara Miles, Sister Gwen Davis, Sister LaJuan Hawkins, Sister Elnora LeGrande, Sister Zina Jones, Sister Carolyn Barnes, Sister Kathy Dent, Sister Sarah F. Rhodes, Brother Billy Webb, Brother Clifford Padgett, Sister Horacestine Miller, Sister Sharon Jones, Sister Gail Pinckney,

Brother Allen Pinckney, Sister Barbara Pinckney, Sister Arcelia Thompson, Sister IraJean Harper, Deacon Warren and Dr. Wendy Edmonds, the late Sister Sylvia Frazier and the Frazier Family, Deacon Nigel John, Deacon Vaughn and Sister Michele Judd, Deacon Lawrence and Sister Hope Smith, Minister Jim, Sister Renee, and Josiah Williamson, Debra Mickens, Charlotte Jennings, Cheryl Jones, Ida Williams, Wilfred Mensah, Sister Blanche Drakeford, Uncle Snipe, Aunt Lucille and children, Uncle James and Aunt Eartha Spellman and children, Pastor Chine Livingston and Aunt Gladys and children, Uncle James and Aunt Rosa Hall and children, Pastor Vernell Hall and children, Dr. John and Sister Christina Thompson and Family, Deacon Charles R. Williams, Sister Gwendolyn McDowell, Brother Claude Jennings (WGTS 91.9 FM, Takoma Maryland) and Cierra Jennings, Pastors Dennit Sr. and Mary Goodwin, Pastor Dennit Goodwin Jr., Sister Tabatha and children, Psalmist Giles and Gayle Cooke and family, Brother John Lewis, both the late Deacon Maurice Contee and Sister Jean Contee, Deacon James E. McCollum Jr. esq., Sister Jameille McMorris, Brother Robert and Gina Aikens, Deacon Riley and Sister Sheila Gaines, Minister Lynette Marie Malbon, Deacon Johnny and Theresa DuBose, Evangelists James and Monique Hickenbottom, Pastors Arthur and Pat Holsey, Sister Monica McDowell, Minister David Whitfield and Psalmist Felece Whitfield, Deacon Ray and Cynthia Smith, Earl Conley, Deacon Wayne Wood and Wife, Deacon Kevin and Sister Monica Hawkins, Nikki Marchal, Sister Deon, Sister Keysha Nelson, the Poole Family, the Welcher Family, Sister Angela Norwood, Deacon George and India Soodoo, the Spivey Family, Stephanie Alston, Deacon Rex and Janice McAllister and Family, Deacon and Sister Darnita Massey, Mother Mamie Green, Lueby, Deacon Donald Green, Clifford Green and "Scooby", Brother Bernard Redfern, Mr. Derrick M. Johnson and Joeralyn White, Ms. Sheran Nimblett, Anthony Wingfield, Charles White IV, Virgilio Ventura, Jovan Robinson, John DeVille, Eric Fuller, Archana Vemulapalli, Rosalyn McKine, Carol Washington, Terrence Goines, Tonishia McAllister, Rithy Lim, Daniel Tauch, Abdul Sesay, Syam Pilli, Raju Penumatchu, Himan Baroi, Tonya Tart, Howard Barrett, Jonquil Prophet, Nathaniel McNair, Beruk Berhanu, Paul Fowler, Keeshia Morse, Theresa Yarborough-Jones, Martha Walls, Jayme Harper, Janice White, Suneel Cherkuri, Mahzar Hamayun, Ken Hall, Raul R. Edwards, Michele Tapp Roseman, Mnkande Shunda, Thaddeus

Hodge, Shirley Daniels, Christina Harper, Jacqueline Brown, Deacon John Cook and Wife, Catherine Gant, Joel Backus, Sister Angela (Goldson) Johnson, Sister Melody Roots, Andre and Derek Dean, Brother Turner and Sister Sabrina Turner, Sister Sonya Cobb, Brother Michael Roberson, Derrick and Victoria Givens, Carolyn Barnes, Julie Plush, Minister Gerald and Pastor Dale Bell, Pastor Richard Williams and Wife, Minister Henry and Sister Sheila Hightower, Carol A. Walker, Faith Sharpe, Wanda Lofton, Harry Gough, Otis Wonsley, Roger Mason Jr., Sister Marsha Augustbaby, Diane P. Crawley, Yolanda Haywood, W Bernard Davis, Sister Dolores and Sister Erica Burgin, Sister Vivian and the Late Deacon Nat Wilson, Covell Johnson, Cornelius Johnson and Family, Brother Deacon and Sister Sherell Williams, Deacon G Vernon White, Deacon Ernest and Ann Lewis, Brother Eric, LaShon, Trinity, Tiffany, Noah and Gabriella (My Goddaughter) Bland, Bishop "Big Willie" McGhee, Minister Wesley and Rosalind Smith, Sister Ann Ivey, Sister Rochelle Langley and family, Brother Gregory and Sister Robin Kelly, the late Cyril Williams Sr., Cyril Williams Jr., Lamar Williams, the late Bradley Jackson, Stanley Jackson, Calvin Burgess, Sr. and Jr., Natalie "IROCLOCS", Tommy Snipe, the Late Maurice Snipe and the rest of the Snipe children and grandchildren, Ismael Sanders and family, DeMarco Lucas and Wife and family, Justin Taylor and Wife, Cody Mackie and Wife and family, Aaron and Chanelle Burt and family, Susie Holloway, Barry Watson, Joseph J. Johnson Sr., Thomas Barnett, Mike Matessino, Jeff Holtz, My Dobbs Ferry Basketball Teammates, George Sweeting, Amie Ziner, Linda and Darlene Spivey, Eric and Maurice Hollis, Sherrie Pastures, Jed Varanelli, Teresa Gelsi, Kathy Farrell, Carol Cunningham, Mark Bingham, Nancy Sacks, Clinton Frank, Haynes Charles, Jim Lindsay, Treacy Crowley, Susan Blunda, Sydney Marks, Diane Dwyer, Nate Roseboro, Michael Farano, Susan Stofsky, Sharon Bowe and Husband, Eileen D. Reader, John Walter, Tarsha and Tameka Roseboro, Rosalie Branch, Michael Rhodie, Susan Todd, Judy Moccia, Margarita Feliciano, Brother Roy and Sister Dawna Parks, Josh Parker, Sister Amanda and Brother Eric Bond, Chianti Tucker, Sivester Washington and family, Martin Luckett, Joyce McPherson, David Cooper, Jeff Bryce, Madeleine Denise (Jones) Jackson, Dennis Jackson, Neil Jones, Phyllis Godette, Gillian Caruth-hunt, Carolyn Starks Norvell, Laurent Marchal, Calvin Neider, Stephanie Seldon, Phyllis Ann and Philipee(sp), Wanda Snipe, and to all my cousins, Evan Rosenberg,

Phillip Stone, Mike Pavlov, Dave Campo, Cathy Cirillo, John Kawalchuk, David Cornell and the late Ivan Cornell, Bill Brennan, Virginia Dix, Lena Thompson, Deacon and Coressa Williams, Lyndon Grey, Pastor Barbara and Deacon Robert Wood, Pastor Samuel Taylor Sr., Pastor Leuvenia and Pastor "Jay" Taylor Jr. and Family (Hi Star), Pastor Gary and Alice Gray, Pastors Jonathan and Lila Smalls, the Smalls sons and daughter, Pastor Johnny Peterson and Wife and family, Brother Deacon Clarence Murray, Elder John Nelson and his late Wife Mary Nelson, the late Bishop Nehemiah Rhinehart, Darren Sheffield, Bro. Artemus "Mike" Bailey, Brother Arnold Goodman, Deacon Curtis and Sister Monica Leonard, Sister Joyce Brooks, cousins Dino and Mike Livingston, Kevin Gentry (Philmark Motorcars) and Wife, Deacon Eduardo Dudley, Sister Judy Spencer, Sister Wanda Pfeiffer, Sister Bernetta Davis, Sister Edith Pyle, Minister Ernie and Mary Ingram, Sister Brenda Williams, Sister Marvena Simmonds, Sister Helen Jamison, Deacon Reggie Harris, Sister Alice Logan, Sister Shirley Joyner, Missionary Madeline Leach, Bishop Vasconcellas Smith and family, David Branch esq. and family, the Late Kenny Williams and Sister Diane Williams, Darryl Williams, Linda Wright and Denise (of GMBC, Bunn, NC), Vernice Green, Lyndon Ardel Joseph, Pastor Ellis Hodges, and Father John of So Others Might Eat (SOME), Washington DC.

*In the event that there is a name of a person that appears in these acknowledgements that have gone on to be with the Lord, I send my apologies for not being privy to such information and also send my condolences out to their loved ones.

**And to all those that I have inadvertently overlooked, it was my head that failed, not my heart. God bless.

Introduction

The Bible of Bible Questions is a collection of questions asked in the Bible itself, from the very first, which appears in Genesis 3:1, to the very last question, which appears in Revelation 17:7. Amazingly enough, the answers to mankind's most elusive questions, concerning God, Jesus, the Holy Spirit, creation, life, death, Satan, the grave and eternity can all be found in The Bible of Bible Questions.

Concerning the more than 3,300 verses recorded in The Bible of Bible Questions; the reader will be able, if they desire, to accurately total the number of questions that appear in the Bible, whether by chapter, by book, or by major division. Imagine being able to determine, who asked the most questions in the Bible? Or, what the longest worded question is in the Bible, and not only how many verses that question occupied while being asked, but also, who asked such a lengthy question, and why? Have you ever considered whether there is a book in the Bible that doesn't have a question asked in it at all? If so; is that book found in the Old Testament or is it found in the New Testament? Or, are there books without questions in both Testaments? Whether for historical or for personal reasons, wouldn't it be interesting to know how many total books there are that don't have questions asked in them? How about being able to determine the number of questions that Jesus himself asked in the Bible; or to be able to uncover, the relationship between two questions asked by Jesus after he was introduced to the temple and after being introduced to the masses? Lastly, how awesome would it be to discover that there is a direct connection between the first question in Genesis to that of the last question in Revelation? Well, as a result of The Bible of Bible Questions, the first and the last question in the Bible are found to be definitively connected, although one occurred in earth and the other in heaven. Hence: "...in earth, as it is in heaven." Matthew 6:9. Divine, I ask, or coincidence?

As The Bible of Bible Questions is studied, one will arrive at some marvelous and wondrous revelations, as of yet hidden; and would continue to be so, if not for this book. Like for example, the definite relationship in the form of questions, that occur in two of the four gospels. In Luke, Jesus was introduced to the Temple at the age of 12 years old and in the gospel of John, he was introduced to the masses, when he was 30 years old. The initial questions posed by Jesus after these separate introductions, both occur as a direct and divine result of Jesus being sought. In Luke 2:49, Jesus asked, How is it that ye sought me? And in John 1:37, Jesus asked, What seek ye? I ask again, divine or coincidence?

Readers will be interested in The Bible of Bible Questions because it is a fascinating and a fashionably relevant topic, which is under-researched and overlooked. The leverage and luxury that such a book would afford any reader, whether casual or professional, whether a teacher or a preacher, whether a psychologist or a sociologist, is possible only by one's respective desire, and determination to hear from heaven on earth. The possibilities of a book as such, are phenomenal; for these questions are able to infuse communication, whether from a pulpit or from a park bench, as they relate to contemporary actions (or lack thereof), events and messages that address the strains that individuals, as well as societies encounter periodically, whether intentionally or ignorantly.

There are answers to everyday concerns, in the form of questions, that permeate the pages of the Bible, that if and when these (the questions) are boldly articulated and addressed in today's times, more likely from a Pastor or from a podium; they would cut to the very quick, not to some of, but to all of the dysfunctionalities prevalent in mankind's warped ideologies today.

Several years ago, while reading through the Bible, I became curious as to the first words which were spoken by Jesus in the gospel of John (the gospel book that intentionally identifies the man Jesus, as also being divine). When I located Jesus' initial recorded conversation in John 1:38; I became intrigued that his first words on record in John were in the form of a question, which, like the definition of the word question itself denotes, was asked with the intent to evoke or to draw out information.

The intent of The Bible of Bible Questions is not only to evoke or draw out information, but is also written to introduce its readers to the 3,300 plus questions that are posed in the Holy Bible, without voluntarily contributing any commentary, interpretation, persuasion or accommodation. In today's age of "social media", simple can be read as sophisticated.

One of the purposes of The Bible of Bible Questions is to capture and maintain the integrity and the innocence (or the lack thereof) of the questions being revisited therein. The Bible of Bible Questions contents will draw one's imagination to the very threshing floor of individuality, concerning either response or restraint.

Can answers, even to life's "terminal" conditions, be found in the questions contained in the Holy Bible; which are captured in The Bible of Bible Questions? And the answer is, unequivocally, yes! For example; suppose an individual asked for proof that there is a God in heaven. What question(s) in the Bible (of Bible Questions) would answer such an inquiry? In the book of Isaiah in chapter 40:21, it asks; "Have ye not known? have ye not heard? hath it not been told you from the beginning? have ye not understood from the foundations of the earth?" and then in Job 22:12 it asks, "Is not God in the height of heaven?"

In The Bible of Bible Questions, it matters less who asked, in Galatians 4:16, "Am I therefore become your enemy, because I tell you the truth?", than it does that the question was ever asked at all. I'm apt to believe that the majority of persons' reaction to a question as such, would be more to the mere timelessness of it, and not so much, initially, as to whom its author was. "Can that which is unsavory be eaten without salt? or is there any taste in the white of an egg?," Job 6:6.

Where else can mankind find a consolidation of definite answers, in the form of questions, concerning things that pertain to life and godliness, except in The Bible of Bible Questions?

Overall, the questions in the Bible have come to inconspicuously navigate themselves through the very fabric of the modern day church. But why are some questions more apt to be remembered by it's members than others? Is it because some are less challenging to remember than others, due to their lack of complexity or profundity? Or, are others more memorable because of their intimacy and proximity to our heart of hearts and life situations? Whichever the case; it's a fact that we remember some questions more readily or even more aggressively than others. "Is there no balm in Gilead; is there no physician there?" Jer. 8:22.

The Bible of Bible Questions, is a collection and consolidation of every question (and only the questions themselves) asked in the Holy Bible, from the book of Genesis through that of Revelation. Whether lengthy for clarity or concise for acuity, all have been captured as such, not so much as to be remembered, as they are to be experienced; rendering the reader to never view the questions contained in the Holy Bible the same way again.

At the time, when I eventually came to realize that what I had first thought to be a hobby, was methodically morphing into a book; I became and remain humbled, that such an historic endeavor, has been entrusted to myself by Almighty God... "And what wisdom is this which is given unto him, that even such mighty works are wrought by his hands?" Mark 6:2

The Bible of Bible Questions; now, henceforth and forever more. Enjoy!

LAW

Come in, thou blessed of the LORD; wherefore standest thou without?
Genesis 24:31

The First Book of Moses Called
Genesis

3:1 Yea, hath God said, Ye shall not eat of every tree of the garden?

3:9 And the LORD God called unto Adam, and said unto him, Where art thou?

3:11 And he said, Who told thee that thou wast naked?

3:11 Hast thou eaten of the tree, whereof I commanded thee that thou shouldest not eat?

3:13 What is this that thou hast done?

4:6 Why art thou wroth?

4:6 Why is thy countenance fallen?

4:7 If thou doest well, shalt thou not be accepted?

4:9 Where is Abel thy brother?

4:9 Am I my brother's keeper?

4:10 What hast thou done?

12:18 What is this that thou hast done unto me?

12:18 Why didst thou not tell me that she was thy wife?

12:19 Why saidst thou, She is my sister?

13:9 Is not the whole land before thee?

15:2 And Abram said, Lord GOD, what wilt thou give me, seeing I go childless, and the steward of my house is this Eliezer of Damascus?

15:8 And he said, Lord GOD, whereby shall I know that I shall inherit it?

16:8 And he said, Hagar, Sarai's maid, whence camest thou?

16:8 Whither wilt thou go?

16:13 Have I also here looked after him that seeth me?

17:17 Shall a child be born unto him that is an hundred years old?

17:17 And shall Sarah, that is ninety years old, bear?

18:9 Where is Sarah thy wife?

18:12 After I am waxed old shall I have pleasure, my lord being old also?

18:13 Wherefore did Sarah laugh, saying, Shall I of a surety bear a child, which am old?

18:14 Is any thing too hard for the LORD?

18:17, 18 And the LORD said, Shall I hide from Abraham that thing which I do; Seeing that Abraham shall surely become a great and mighty nation, and all the nations of the earth shall be blessed in him?

18:23 Wilt thou also destroy the righteous with the wicked?

18:24 Peradventure there be fifty righteous within the city: wilt thou also destroy and not spare the place for the fifty righteous that are therein?

18:25 Shall not the Judge of all the earth do right?

18:28 Peradventure there shall lack five of the fifty righteous: wilt thou destroy all the city for lack of five?

19:5 Where are the men which came in to thee this night?

19:12 And the men said unto Lot, Hast thou here any besides?

19:20 Behold now, this city is near to flee unto, and it is a little one: Oh, let me escape thither, (is it not a little one?) and my soul shall live.

20:4 Lord, wilt thou slay also a righteous nation?

20:5 Said he not unto me, She is my sister?

20:9 Then Abimelech called Abraham, and said unto him, What hast thou done unto us?

20:9 And what have I offended thee, that thou hast brought on me and on my kingdom a great sin?

20:10 What sawest thou, that thou hast done this thing?

21:7 Who would have said unto Abraham, that Sarah should have given children suck?

21:17 What aileth thee, Hagar?

21:29 What mean these seven ewe lambs which thou hast set by themselves?

22:7 Behold the fire and the wood: but where is the lamb for a burnt offering?

23:15 My lord, hearken unto me: the land is worth four hundred shekels of silver; what is that betwixt me and thee? bury therefore thy dead.

24:5 Peradventure the woman will not be willing to follow me unto this land: must I needs bring thy son again unto the land from whence thou camest?

24:23 Whose daughter art thou?

24:23 Is there room in thy father's house for us to lodge in?

24:31 Come in, thou blessed of the LORD; wherefore standest thou without?

24:47 And I asked her, and said, Whose daughter art thou? And she said, The daughter of Bethuel, Nahor's son, whom Milcah bare unto him: and I put the earring upon her face, and the bracelets upon her hands.

24:58 Wilt thou go with this man?

24:65 For she had said unto the servant, What man is this that walketh in the field to meet us? And the servant had said, It is my master: therefore she took a vail, and covered herself.

25:22 If it be so, why am I thus?

25:32 And what profit shall this birthright do to me?

26:9 Behold, of a surety she is thy wife: and how saidst thou, She is my sister?

26:10 What is this thou hast done unto us?

26:27 Wherefore come ye to me, seeing ye hate me, and have sent me away from you?

27:18 Who art thou, my son?

27:20 How is it that thou hast found it so quickly, my son?

27:24 Art thou my very son Esau?

27:32 Who art thou?

27:33 Who?

27:33 Where is he that hath taken venison, and brought it me, and I have eaten of all before thou camest, and have blessed him?

27:36 Is not he rightly named Jacob?

27:36 Hast thou not reserved a blessing for me?

27:37 And with corn and wine have I sustained him: and what shall I do now unto thee, my son?

27:38 Hast thou but one blessing, my father?

27:45 Why should I be deprived also of you both in one day?

27:46 What good shall my life do me?

29:4 And Jacob said unto them, My brethren, whence be ye? And they said, Of Haran are we.

29:5 And he said unto them, Know ye Laban the son of Nahor? And they said, We know him.

29:6 And he said unto them, Is he well? And they said, He is well: and, behold, Rachel his daughter cometh with the sheep.

29:15 And Laban said unto Jacob, Because thou art my brother, shouldest thou therefore serve me for nought?

29:15 Tell me, what shall thy wages be?

29:25 And it came to pass, that in the morning, behold, it was Leah: and he said to Laban, What is this thou hast done unto me?

29:25 Did not I serve with thee for Rachel?

29:25 Wherefore then hast thou beguiled me?

30:2 And Jacob's anger was kindled against Rachel: and he said, Am I in God's stead, who hath withheld from thee the fruit of the womb?

30:15 And she said unto her, Is it a small matter that thou hast taken my husband?

30:15 And wouldest thou take away my son's mandrakes also?

30:30 For it was little which thou hadst before I came, and it is now increased unto a multitude; and the LORD hath blessed thee since my coming: and now when shall I provide for mine own house also?

30:31 And he said, What shall I give thee? And Jacob said, Thou shalt not give me any thing: if thou wilt do this thing for me, I will again feed and keep thy flock.

31:14 And Rachel and Leah answered and said unto him, Is there yet any portion or inheritance for us in our father's house?

31:15 Are we not counted of him strangers? for he hath sold us, and hath quite devoured also our money.

31:26 And Laban said to Jacob, What hast thou done, that thou hast stolen away unawares to me, and carried away my daughters, as captives taken with the sword?

31:27 Wherefore didst thou flee away secretly, and steal away from me; and didst not tell me, that I might have sent thee away with mirth, and with songs, with tabret, and with harp?

31:28 And hast not suffered me to kiss my sons and my daughters? thou hast now done foolishly in so doing.

31:30 And now, though thou wouldest needs be gone, because thou sore longedst after thy father's house, yet wherefore hast thou stolen my gods?

31:36 What is my trespass?

31:36 What is my sin, that thou hast so hotly pursued after me?

31:37 Whereas thou hast searched all my stuff, what hast thou found of all thy household stuff?

31:43 What can I do this day unto these my daughters, or unto their children which they have born?

32:17 Whose art thou?

32:17 And whither goest thou?

32:17 And whose are these before thee?

32:27 What is thy name?

32:29 Wherefore is it that thou dost ask after my name?

33:5 Who are those with thee?

33:8 What meanest thou by all this drove which I met?

33:15 What needeth it?

34:23 Shall not their cattle and their substance and every beast of theirs be ours?

34:31 Should he deal with our sister as with an harlot?

37:8 Shalt thou indeed reign over us?

37:8 Or shalt thou indeed have dominion over us?

37:10 What is this dream that thou hast dreamed?

37:10 Shall I and thy mother and thy brethren indeed come to bow down ourselves to thee to the earth?

37:13 Do not thy brethren feed the flock in Shechem?

37:15 What seekest thou?

37:26 What profit is it if we slay our brother, and conceal his blood?

37:30 And I, whither shall I go?

38:16 What wilt thou give me, that thou mayest come in unto me?

38:17 Wilt thou give me a pledge, till thou send it?

38:18 What pledge shall I give thee?

38:21 Where is the harlot, that was openly by the way side?

38:21 Where is the harlot, that was openly by the way side? And they said, There was no harlot in this place.

38:29 How hast thou broken forth?

39:9 How then can I do this great wickedness, and sin against God?

40:7 Wherefore look ye so sadly to day?

40:8 Do not interpretations belong to God?

41:38 Can we find such a one as this is, a man in whom the Spirit of God is?

42:1 Why do ye look one upon another?

42:7 Whence come ye?

42:22 Spake I not unto you, saying, Do not sin against the child; and ye would not hear?

42:28 What is this that God hath done unto us?

43:6 Wherefore dealt ye so ill with me, as to tell the man whether ye had yet a brother?

43:7 Is your father yet alive?

43:7 Have ye another brother?

43:7 Could we certainly know that he would say, Bring your brother down?

43:27 Is your father well, the old man of whom ye spake?

43:27 Is he yet alive?

43:29 Is this your younger brother, of whom ye spake unto me?

44:4 Wherefore have ye rewarded evil for good?

44:7 Wherefore saith my lord these words?

44:8 How then should we steal out of thy lord's house silver or gold?

44:15 What deed is this that ye have done?

44:15 Wot ye not that such a man as I can certainly divine?

44:16 What shall we say unto my lord?

44:16 What shall we speak?

44:16 Or how shall we clear ourselves?

44:19 Have ye a father, or a brother?

44:34 For how shall I go up to my father, and the lad be not with me?

45:3 Doth my father yet live?

46:33 What is your occupation?

47:3 What is your occupation?

47:8 How old art thou?

47:15 Give us bread: for why should we die in thy presence?

48:8 Who are these?

49:9 Who shall rouse him up?

50:19 Fear not: for am I in the place of God?

The Second Book of Moses Called
Exodus

1:18 Why have ye done this thing, and have saved the men children alive?

2:7 Shall I go and call to thee of the Hebrew women, that she may nurse the child for thee?

2:13 Wherefore smitest thou thy fellow?

2:14 Who made thee a prince and a judge over us?

2:14 Intendest thou to kill me, as thou killedst the Egyptian?

2:18 How is it that ye are come so soon to day?

2:20 Where is he?

2:20 Why is it that ye have left the man? call him, that he may eat bread.

3:11 Who am I, that I should go unto Pharaoh, and that I should bring forth the children of Israel out of Egypt?

3:13 Behold, when I come unto the children of Israel, and shall say unto them, The God of your fathers hath sent me unto you; and they shall say to me, What is his name?

3:13 What shall I say unto them?

4:2 What is that in thine hand?

4:11 Who hath made man's mouth?

4:11 Who maketh the dumb, or deaf, or the seeing, or the blind?

4:11 Have not I the LORD?

4:14 Is not Aaron the Levite thy brother?

5:2 Who is the LORD, that I should obey his voice to let Israel go?

5:4 Wherefore do ye, Moses and Aaron, let the people from their works?

5:14 Wherefore have ye not fulfilled your task in making brick both yesterday and to day, as heretofore?

5:15 Wherefore dealest thou thus with thy servants?

5:22 Wherefore hast thou so evil entreated this people?

5:22 Why is it that thou hast sent me?

6:12 How then shall Pharaoh hear me, who am of uncircumcised lips?

6:30 And Moses said before the LORD, Behold, I am of uncircumcised lips, and how shall Pharaoh hearken unto me?

8:9 When shall I intreat for thee, and for thy servants, and for thy people, to destroy the frogs from thee and thy houses, that they may remain in the river only?

8:26 Shall we sacrifice the abomination of the Egyptians before their eyes, and will they not stone us?

9:17 Exaltest thou thyself against my people, that thou wilt not let them go?

10:3 How long wilt thou refuse to humble thyself before me?

10:7 How long shall this man be a snare unto us?

10:7 Let the men go, that they may serve the LORD their God: knowest thou not yet that Egypt is destroyed?

10:8 Go, serve the LORD your God: but who are they that shall go?

12:26 And it shall come to pass, when your children shall say unto you, What mean ye by this service?

13:14 When thy son asketh thee in time to come, saying what is this?

14:5 Why have we done this, that we have let Israel go from serving us?

14:11 Because there were no graves in Egypt, hast thou taken us away to die in the wilderness?

14:11 Wherefore hast thou dealt thus with us, to carry us forth out of Egypt?

14:12 Is not this the word that we did tell thee in Egypt, saying, Let us alone, that we may serve the Egyptians?

14:15 Wherefore criest thou unto me?

15:11 Who is like unto thee, O LORD, among the gods?

15:11 Who is like thee, glorious in holiness, fearful in praises, doing wonders?

15:24 What shall we drink?

16:7 What are we, that ye murmur against us?

16:8 The LORD heareth your murmurings which ye murmur against him: and what are we? your murmurings are not against us, but against the LORD.

16:28 How long refuse ye to keep my commandments and my laws?

17:2 Why chide [quarrel] ye with me?

17:2 Wherefore do ye tempt the LORD?

17:3 Wherefore is this that thou hast brought us up out of Egypt, to kill us and our children and our cattle with thirst?

17:4 And Moses cried unto the LORD, saying, What shall I do unto this people? they be almost ready to stone me.

17:7 Is the LORD among us, or not?

18:14 What is this thing that thou doest to the people?

18:14 Why sittest thou thyself alone, and all the people stand by thee from morning unto even?

22:27 Wherein shall he sleep?

32:11 Why doth thy wrath wax hot against thy people, which thou hast brought forth out of the land of Egypt with great power, and with a mighty hand?

32:12 Wherefore should the Egyptians speak, and say, For mischief did he bring them out, to slay them in the mountains, and to consume them from the face of the earth?

32:21 What did this people unto thee, that thou hast brought so great a sin upon them?

32:26 Who is on the LORD'S side?

33:16 For wherein shall it be known here that I and thy people have found grace in thy sight?

33:16 Is it not in that thou goest with us?

The Third Book of Moses Called
Leviticus

10:17 Wherefore have ye not eaten the sin offering in the holy place, seeing it is most holy, and God hath given it you to bear the iniquity of the congregation, to make atonement for them before the LORD?

10:19 And Aaron said unto Moses, Behold, this day have they offered their sin offering and their burnt offering before the LORD; and such things have befallen me: and if I had eaten the sin offering to day, should it have been accepted in the sight of the LORD?

25:20 What shall we eat the seventh year?

The Fourth Book of Moses Called
Numbers

9:7 We are defiled by the dead body of a man: wherefore are we kept back, that we may not offer an offering of the LORD in his appointed season among the children of Israel?

11:4 And the mixt multitude that was among them fell a lusting: and the children of Israel also wept again, and said, Who shall give us flesh to eat?

11:11 Wherefore hast thou afflicted thy servant?

11:11 And wherefore have I not found favour in thy sight, that thou layest the burden of all this people upon me?

11:12 Have I conceived all this people?

11:12 Have I begotten them, that thou shouldest say unto me, Carry them in thy bosom, as a nursing father beareth the sucking child, unto the land which thou swarest unto their fathers?

11:13 Whence should I have flesh to give unto all this people?

11:18 For ye have wept in the ears of the LORD, saying, Who shall give us flesh to eat?

11:20 Ye have despised the LORD which is among you, and have wept before him, saying, Why came we forth out of Egypt?

11:22 Shall the flocks and the herds be slain for them, to suffice them?

11:22 Or shall all the fish of the sea be gathered together for them, to suffice them?

11:23 Is the LORD'S hand waxed short?

12:2 Hath the LORD indeed spoken only by Moses?

12:2 Hath he not spoken also by us?

12:8 Wherefore then were ye not afraid to speak against my servant Moses?

12:14 If her father had but spit in her face, should she not be ashamed seven days?

14:3 And wherefore hath the LORD brought us unto this land, to fall by the sword, that our wives and our children should be a prey?

14:3 Were it not better for us to return into Egypt?

14:11 How long will this people provoke me?

14:11 And how long will it be ere they believe me, for all the signs which I have shewed among them?

14:27 How long shall I bear with this evil congregation, which murmur against me?

14:41 Wherefore now do ye transgress the commandment of the LORD?

16:3 Wherefore then lift ye up yourselves above the congregation of the LORD?

16:9 Seemeth it but a small thing unto you, that the God of Israel hath separated you from the congregation of Israel, to bring you near to himself to do the service of the tabernacle of the LORD, and to stand before the congregation to minister unto them?

16:10 Seek ye the priesthood also?

16:11 For which cause both thou and all thy company are gathered together against the LORD: and what is Aaron, that ye murmur against him?

16:13 Is it a small thing that thou hast brought us up out of a land that floweth with milk and honey, to kill us in the wilderness, except thou make thyself altogether a prince over us?

16:14 Moreover thou hast not brought us into a land that floweth with milk and honey, or given us inheritance of fields and vineyards: wilt thou put out the eyes of these men?

16:22 O God, the God of the spirits of all flesh, shall one man sin, and wilt thou be wroth with all the congregation?

17:13 Shall we be consumed with dying?

20:4 And why have ye brought up the congregation of the LORD into this wilderness, that we and our cattle should die there?

20:5 And wherefore have ye made us to come up out of Egypt, to bring us in unto this evil place?

20:10 And Moses and Aaron gathered the congregation together before the rock, and he said unto them, Hear now, ye rebels; must we fetch you water out of this rock?

22:9 What men are these with thee?

22:28 What have I done unto thee, that thou hast smitten me these three times?

22:30 And the ass said unto Balaam, Am not I thine ass, upon which thou hast ridden ever since I was thine unto this day?

22:30 Was I ever wont to do so unto thee?

22:32 And the angel of the LORD said unto him, Wherefore hast thou smitten thine ass these three times?

22:37 Did I not earnestly send unto thee to call thee?

22:37 Wherefore camest thou not unto me?

22:37 Am I not able indeed to promote thee to honour?

22:38 And Balaam said unto Balak, Lo, I am come unto thee: have I now any power at all to say any thing? the word that God putteth in my mouth, that shall I speak.

23:8 How shall I curse, whom God hath not cursed?

23:8 Or how shall I defy, whom the LORD hath not defied?

23:10 Who can count the dust of Jacob, and the number of the fourth part of Israel?

23:11 And Balak said unto Balaam, What hast thou done unto me? I took thee to curse mine enemies, and, behold, thou hast blessed them altogether.

23:12 And he answered and said, Must I not take heed to speak that which the LORD hath put in my mouth?

23:17 And Balak said unto him, What hath the LORD spoken?

23:19 God is not a man, that he should lie; neither the son of man, that he should repent: hath he said, and shall he not do it?

23:19 Or hath he spoken, and shall he not make it good?

23:26 Told not I thee, saying, All that the LORD speaketh, that I must do?

24:9 He couched, he lay down as a lion, and as a great lion: who shall stir him up?

24:13 If Balak would give me his house full of silver and gold, I cannot go beyond the commandment of the LORD, to do either good or bad of mine own, but What the LORD saith, that will I speak?

27:4 Why should the name of our father be done away from among his family, because he hath no son?

31:15 Have ye saved all the women alive?

32:6 Shall your brethren go to war, and shall ye sit here?

32:7 And wherefore discourage ye the heart of the children of Israel from going over into the land which the LORD hath given them?

The Fifth Book of Moses Called
Deuteronomy

1:12 How can I myself alone bear your cumbrance, and your burden, and your strife?

1:28 Whither shall we go up?

3:11 For only Og king of Bashan remained of the remnant of giants; behold, his bedstead was a bedstead of iron; is it not in Rabbath of the children of Ammon?

3:24 For what God is there in heaven or in earth, that can do according to thy works, and according to thy might?

4:7 For what nation is there so great, who hath God so nigh unto them, as the LORD our God is in all things that we call upon him for?

4:8 And what nation is there so great, that hath statutes and judgments so righteous as all this law, which I set before you this day?

4:32 Ask from the one side of heaven unto the other, whether there hath been any such thing as this great thing is, or hath been heard like it?

4:33 Did ever people hear the voice of God speaking out of the midst of the fire, as thou hast heard, and live?

4:34 Or hath God assayed to go and take him a nation from the midst of another nation, by temptations, by signs, and by wonders, and by war, and by a mighty hand, and by a stretched out arm, and by great terrors, according to all that the LORD your God did for you in Egypt before your eyes?

5:25 Now therefore why should we die?

5:26 For who is there of all flesh, that hath heard the voice of the living God speaking out of the midst of the fire, as we have, and lived?

6:20 What mean the testimonies, and the statutes, and the judgments, which the LORD our God hath commanded you?

7:17 These nations are more than I; how can I dispossess them?

10:12, 13 What doth the LORD thy God require of thee, but to fear the LORD thy God, to walk in all his ways, and to love him, and to serve the LORD thy God with all thy heart and with all thy soul, To keep the commandments of the LORD, and his statutes, which I command thee this day for thy good?

12:30 How did these nations serve their gods? even so will I do likewise.

18:21 How shall we know the word which the LORD hath not spoken?

20:5 What man is there that hath built a new house, and hath not dedicated it?

20:6 And what man is he that hath planted a vineyard, and hath not yet eaten of it?

20:7 And what man is there that hath betrothed a wife, and hath not taken her?

20:8 What man is there that is fearful and fainthearted?

29:24 Wherefore hath the LORD done thus unto this land?

29:24 What meaneth the heat of this great anger?

30:12 Who shall go up for us to heaven, and bring it unto us, that we may hear it, and do it?

30:13 Who shall go over the sea for us, and bring it unto us, that we may hear it, and do it?

31:17 Are not these evils come upon us, because our God is not among us?

31:27 Ye have been rebellious against the LORD; and how much more after my death?

32:6 Do ye thus requite the LORD, O foolish people and unwise?

32:6 Is not he thy father that hath bought thee?

32:6 Hath he not made thee, and established thee?

32:30 How should one chase a thousand, and two put ten thousand to flight, except their Rock had sold them, and the LORD had shut them up?

32:34 Is not this laid up in store with me, and sealed up among my treasures?

32:37, 38 Where are their gods, their rock in whom they trusted, Which did eat the fat of their sacrifices, and drank the wine of their drink offerings?

HISTORY

*How long are ye slack to go to possess the land, which
the LORD God of your fathers hath given thee?
Joshua 18:3*

The Book of
Joshua

1:9 Have not I commanded thee? Be strong and of a good courage; be not afraid, neither be thou dismayed: for the LORD thy God is with thee whithersoever thou goest.

4:6 What mean ye by these stones?

4:21 What mean these stones?

7:7 Alas, O Lord GOD, wherefore hast thou at all brought this people over Jordan, to deliver us into the hand of the Amorites, to destroy us?

7:9 What wilt thou do unto thy great name?

7:10 Wherefore liest thou thus upon thy face?

7:25 Why hast thou troubled us?

9:7 Peradventure ye dwell among us; and how shall we make a league with you?

9:8 Who are ye?

9:8 And from whence come ye?

9:22 Wherefore have ye beguiled us, saying, We are very far from you; when ye dwell among us?

10:13 Is not this written in the book of Jasher? So the sun stood still in the midst of heaven, and hasted not to go down about a whole day.

15:18 What wouldest thou?

17:14 Why hast thou given me but one lot and one portion to inherit, seeing I am a great people, forasmuch as the LORD hath blessed me hitherto?

18:3 How long are ye slack to go to possess the land, which the LORD God of your fathers hath given you?

22:24 What have ye to do with the LORD God of Israel?

The Book of
Judges

1:1 Who shall go up for us against the Canaanites first, to fight against them?

1:14 What wilt thou?

2:2 Why have ye done this?

4:6 Hath not the LORD God of Israel commanded, saying, Go and draw toward mount Tabor, and take with thee ten thousand men of the children of Naphtali and of the children of Zebulun?

4:14 Is not the LORD gone out before thee?

4:20 Is there any man here?

5:8 Was there a shield or spear seen among forty thousand in Israel?

5:16 Why abodest thou among the sheepfolds, to hear the bleatings of the flocks?

5:17 Why did Dan remain in ships?

5:28 Why is his chariot so long in coming?

5:28 Why tarry the wheels of his chariots?

5:30 Have they not sped?

5:30 Have they not divided the prey; to every man a damsel or two; to Sisera a prey of divers colours, a prey of divers colours of needlework, of divers colours of needlework on both sides, meet for the necks of them that take the spoil?

6:13 Oh my Lord, if the LORD be with us, why then is all this befallen us?

6:13 And where be all his miracles which our fathers told us of, saying, Did not the LORD bring us up from Egypt?

6:14 Go in this thy might, and thou shalt save Israel from the hand of the Midianites: have not I sent thee?

6:15 Oh my Lord, wherewith shall I save Israel? behold, my family is poor in Manasseh, and I am the least in my father's house.

6:29 Who hath done this thing?

6:31 Will ye plead for Baal?

6:31 Will ye save him?

8:1 Why hast thou served us thus, that thou calledst us not, when thou wentest to fight with the Midianites?

8:2 What have I done now in comparison of you?

8:2 Is not the gleaning of the grapes of Ephraim better than the vintage of Abiezer?

8:3 God hath delivered into your hands the princes of Midian, Oreb and Zeeb: and what was I able to do in comparison of you?

8:6 Are the hands of Zebah and Zalmunna now in thine hand, that we should give bread unto thine army?

8:15 Behold Zebah and Zalmunna, with whom ye did upbraid me, saying, Are the hands of Zebah and Zalmunna now in thine hand, that we should give bread unto thy men that are weary?

8:18 What manner of men were they whom ye slew at Tabor?

9:2 Whether is better for you, either that all the sons of Jerubbaal, which are threescore and ten persons, reign over you, or that one reign over you?

9:9 Should I leave my fatness, wherewith by me they honour God and man, and go to be promoted over the trees?

9:11 Should I forsake my sweetness, and my good fruit, and go to be promoted over the trees?

9:13 Should I leave my wine, which cheereth God and man, and go to be promoted over the trees?

9:28 Who is Abimelech, and who is Shechem, that we should serve him?

9:28 Is not he the son of Jerubbaal?

9:28 And Zebul his officer?

9:28 Why should we serve him?

9:38 Where is now thy mouth, wherewith thou saidst, Who is Abimelech, that we should serve him?

9:38 Is not this the people that thou hast despised?

10:11 Did not I deliver you from the Egyptians, and from the Amorites, from the children of Ammon, and from the Philistines?

10:18 What man is he that will begin to fight against the children of Ammon?

11:7 Did not ye hate me, and expel me out of my father's house?

11:7 And why are ye come unto me now when ye are in distress?

11:9 If ye bring me home again to fight against the children of Ammon, and the LORD deliver them before me, shall I be your head?

11:12 What hast thou to do with me, that thou art come against me to fight in my land?

11:23 So now the LORD God of Israel hath dispossessed the Amorites from before his people Israel, and shouldest thou possess it?

11:24 Wilt not thou possess that which Chemosh thy god giveth thee to possess?

11:25 Art thou any thing better than Balak the son of Zippor, king of Moab? Did he ever strive against Israel, or did he ever fight them.

11:26 While Israel dwelt in Heshbon and her towns, and in Aroer and her towns, and in all the cities that be along by the coasts of Arnon, three hundred years?

11:26 Why therefore did ye not recover them within that time?

12:1 Wherefore passedst thou over to fight against the children of Ammon, and didst not call us to go with thee?

12:3 Wherefore then are ye come up unto me this day, to fight against me?

12:5 Art thou an Ephraimite?

13:11 Art thou the man that spakest unto the woman?

13:12 How shall we order the child, and how shall we do unto him?

13:17 What is thy name, that when thy sayings come to pass we may do thee honour?

13:18 Why askest thou thus after my name, seeing it is secret?

14:3 Is there never a woman among the daughters of thy brethren, or among all my people, that thou goest to take a wife of the uncircumcised Philistines?

14:15 Have ye called us to take that we have?

14:15 Is it not so?

14:16 Behold, I have not told it my father nor my mother, and shall I tell it thee?

14:18 What is sweeter than honey?

14:18 And what is stronger than a lion?

15:2 Is not her younger sister fairer than she? take her, I pray thee, instead.

15:6 Who hath done this?

15:10 Why are ye come up against us?

15:11 Knowest thou not that the Philistines are rulers over us? what is this that thou hast.

15:11 What is this that thou hast done unto us?

15:18 Thou hast given this great deliverance into the hand of thy servant: and now shall I die for thirst, and fall into the hand of the uncircumcised?

16:15 How canst thou say, I love thee, when thine heart is not with me?

17:9 Whence comest thou?

18:3 Who brought thee hither?

18:3 What makest thou in this place?

18:3 What hast thou here?

18:8 What say ye?

18:9 Arise, that we may go up against them: for we have seen the land, and, behold, it is very good: and are ye still? be not slothful to go, and to enter to possess the land.

18:14 Do ye know that there is in these houses an ephod, and teraphim, and a graven image, and a molten image?

18:18 What do ye?

18:19 Is it better for thee to be a priest unto the house of one man, or that thou be a priest unto a tribe and a family in Israel?

18:23 What aileth thee, that thou comest with such a company?

18:24 Ye have taken away my gods which I made, and the priest, and ye are gone away: and what have I more?

18:24 And what is this that ye say unto me, What aileth thee?

19:17 Whither goest thou?

19:17 And whence comest thou?

20:3 Tell us, how was this wickedness?

20:12 What wickedness is this that is done among you?

20:18 Which of us shall go up first to the battle against the children of Benjamin? And the LORD said, Judah shall go up first.

20:23 Shall I go up again to battle against the children of Benjamin my brother? And the LORD said, Go up against him.

20:28 Shall I yet again go out to battle against the children of Benjamin my brother, or shall I cease? And the LORD said, Go up; for tomorrow I will deliver them into thine hand.

21:3 Why is this come to pass in Israel, that there should be to day one tribe lacking in Israel?

21:5 Who is there among all the tribes of Israel that came not up with the congregation unto the LORD?

21:7 How shall we do for wives for them that remain, seeing we have sworn by the LORD that we will not give them of our daughters to wives?

21:8 What one is there of the tribes of Israel that came not up to Mizpeh to the LORD?

21:16 How shall we do for wives for them that remain, seeing the women are destroyed out of Benjamin?

The Book of
Ruth

1:11 Why will ye go with me?

1:11 Are there yet any more sons in my womb, that they may be your husbands?

1:12, 13 If I should say, I have hope, if I should have an husband also to night, and should also bear sons; Would ye tarry for them till they were grown?

1:13 Would ye stay for them from having husbands?

1:19 Is this Naomi?

1:21 Why then call ye me Naomi, seeing the LORD hath testified against me, and the Almighty hath afflicted me?

2:5 Whose damsel is this?

2:8 Hearest thou not, my daughter?

2:9 Have I not charged the young men that they shall not touch thee?

2:10 Why have I found grace in thine eyes, that thou shouldest take knowledge of me, seeing I am a stranger?

2:19 Where hast thou gleaned to day?

2:19 Where wroughtest thou?

3:1 Shall I not seek rest for thee, that it may be well with thee?

3:2 Is not Boaz of our kindred, with whose maidens thou wast?

3:9 Who art thou?

3:16 Who art thou, my daughter?

The First Book of
Samuel—Otherwise Called
the First Book of the Kings

1:8 Why weepest thou?

1:8 And why eatest thou not?

1:8 And why is thy heart grieved?

1:8 Am not I better to thee than ten sons?

1:14 How long wilt thou be drunken?

2:23 Why do ye such things?

2:25 If one man sin against another, the judge shall judge him: but if a man sin against the LORD, who shall intreat for him?

2:27 Thus saith the LORD, Did I plainly appear unto the house of thy father, when they were in Egypt in Pharaoh's house?

2:28 And did I choose him out of all the tribes of Israel to be my priest, to offer upon mine altar, to burn incense, to wear an ephod before me?

2:28 And did I give unto the house of thy father all the offerings made by fire of the children of Israel?

2:29 Wherefore kick ye at my sacrifice and at mine offering, which I have commanded in my habitation; and honourest thy sons above me, to make yourselves fat with the chiefest of all the offerings of Israel my people?

3:17 What is the thing that the LORD hath said unto thee?

4:3 Wherefore hath the LORD smitten us to day before the Philistines?

4:6 What meaneth the noise of this great shout in the camp of the Hebrews?

4:8 Who shall deliver us out of the hand of these mighty Gods?

4:14 What meaneth the noise of this tumult?

4:16 What is there done, my son?

5:8 What shall we do with the ark of the God of Israel?

6:2 What shall we do to the ark of the LORD?

6:4 What shall be the trespass offering which we shall return to him?

6:6 Wherefore then do ye harden your hearts, as the Egyptians and Pharaoh hardened their hearts?

6:6 When he had wrought wonderfully among them, did they not let the people go, and they departed?

6:20 Who is able to stand before this holy LORD God?

6:20 And to whom shall he go up from us?

9:7 But, behold, if we go, what shall we bring the man?

9:7 For the bread is spent in our vessels, and there is not a present to bring to the man of God: what have we?

9:11 Is the seer here?

9:20 On whom is all the desire of Israel?

9:20 Is it not on thee, and on all thy father's house?

9:21 Am not I a Benjamite, of the smallest of the tribes of Israel?

9:21 And my family the least of all the families of the tribe of Benjamin?

9:21 Wherefore then speakest thou so to me?

10:1 Is it not because the LORD hath anointed thee to be captain over his inheritance?

10:2 What shall I do for my son?

10:11 What is this that is come unto the son of Kish?

10:11 Is Saul also among the prophets?

10:12 But who is their father?

10:12 Therefore it became a proverb, Is Saul also among the prophets?

10:14 Whither went ye?

10:24 See ye him whom the LORD hath chosen, that there is none like him among all the people?

10:27 How shall this man save us?

11:5 What aileth the people that they weep?

11:12 Who is he that said, Shall Saul reign over us?

12:3 Behold, here I am: witness against me before the LORD, and before his anointed: whose ox have I taken?

12:3 Or whose ass have I taken?

12:3 Or whom have I defrauded?

12:3 Whom have I oppressed?

12:3 Or of whose hand have I received any bribe to blind mine eyes therewith?

12:17 Is it not wheat harvest to day?

13:11 What hast thou done?

14:30 How much more, if haply the people had eaten freely to day of the spoil of their enemies which they found?

14:30 For had there not been now a much greater slaughter among the Philistines?

14:30 How much more, if haply the people had eaten freely to day of the spoil of their enemies which they found?

14:30 For had there not been now a much greater slaughter among the Philistines?

14:37 Shall I go down after the Philistines?

14:37 Wilt thou deliver them into the hand of Israel?

14:45 Shall Jonathan die, who hath wrought this great salvation in Israel?

15:14 What meaneth then this bleating of the sheep in mine ears, and the lowing of the oxen which I hear?

15:17 When thou wast little in thine own sight, wast thou not made the head of the tribes of Israel, and the LORD anointed thee king over Israel?

15:19 Wherefore then didst thou not obey the voice of the LORD, but didst fly upon the spoil, and didst evil in the sight of the LORD?

15:22 Hath the LORD as great delight in burnt offerings and sacrifices, as in obeying the voice of the LORD?

16:1 How long wilt thou mourn for Saul, seeing I have rejected him from reigning over Israel?

16:2 How can I go?

16:4 Comest thou peaceably?

16:11 Are here all thy children?

17:8 Why are ye come out to set your battle in array?

17:8 Am not I a Philistine, and ye servants to Saul?

17:25 Have ye seen this man that is come up?

17:26 What shall be done to the man that killeth this Philistine, and taketh away the reproach from Israel?

17:26 For who is this uncircumcised Philistine, that he should defy the armies of the living God?

17:28 Why camest thou down hither?

17:28 And with whom hast thou left those few sheep in the wilderness?

17:29 What have I now done?

17:29 Is there not a cause?

17:43 Am I a dog, that thou comest to me with staves?

17:55 Whose son is this youth?

17:58 Whose son art thou, thou young man?

18:8 They have ascribed unto David ten thousands, and to me they have ascribed but thousands: and what can he have more but the kingdom?

18:18 Who am I?

18:18 And what is my life, or my father's family in Israel, that I should be son in law to the king?

18:23 Seemeth it to you a light thing to be a king's son in law, seeing that I am a poor man, and lightly esteemed?

19:5 Wherefore then wilt thou sin against innocent blood, to slay David without a cause?

19:17 Why hast thou deceived me so, and sent away mine enemy, that he is escaped?

19:17 He said unto me, Let me go; why should I kill thee?

19:22 Where are Samuel and David?

19:24 Wherefore they say, Is Saul also among the prophets?

20:1 What have I done?

20:1 What is mine iniquity?

20:1 And what is my sin before thy father, that he seeketh my life?

20:2 Why should my father hide this thing from me? it is not so.

20:8 Why shouldest thou bring me to thy father?

20:9 For if I knew certainly that evil were determined by my father to come upon thee, then would not I tell it thee?

20:10 Who shall tell me?

20:10 What if thy father answer thee roughly?

20:27 Wherefore cometh not the son of Jesse to meat, neither yesterday, nor to day?

20:30 Thou son of the perverse rebellious woman, do not I know that thou hast chosen the son of Jesse to thine own confusion, and unto the confusion of thy mother's nakedness?

20:32 Wherefore shall he be slain?

20:32 What hath he done?

20:37 Is not the arrow beyond thee?

21:1 Why art thou alone, and no man with thee?

21:3 What is under thine hand?

21:8 And is there not here under thine hand spear or sword?

21:11 Is not this David the king of the land?

21:11 Did they not sing one to another of him in dances, saying, Saul hath slain his thousands, and David his ten thousands?

21:14 Wherefore then have ye brought him to me?

21:15 Have I need of mad men, that ye have brought this fellow to play the mad man in my presence?

21:15 Shall this fellow come into my house?

22:13 Why have ye conspired against me, thou and the son of Jesse, in that thou hast given him bread, and a sword, and hast enquired of God for him, that he should rise against me, to lie in wait, as at this day?

22:14 Who is so faithful among all thy servants as David, which is the king's son in law, and goeth at thy bidding, and is honourable in thine house?

22:15 Did I then begin to enquire of God for him?

22:7, 8 Hear now, ye Benjamites; will the son of Jesse give every one of you fields and vineyards, and make you all captains of thousands, and captains of hundreds; That all of you have conspired against me, and there is none that sheweth me that my son hath made a league with the son of Jesse, and there is none of you that is sorry for me, or sheweth unto me that my son hath stirred up my servant against me, to lie in wait, as at this day?

23:2 Shall I go and smite these Philistines?

23:3 We be afraid here in Judah: how much more then if we come to Keilah against the armies of the Philistines?

23:11 Will the men of Keilah deliver me up into his hand?

23:11 Will Saul come down, as thy servant hath heard?

23:12 Then said David, Will the men of Keilah deliver me and my men into the hand of Saul? And the LORD said, They will deliver thee up.

23:19 Doth not David hide himself with us in strong holds in the wood, in the hill of Hachilah, which is on the south of Jeshimon?

24:9 Wherefore hearest thou men's words, saying, Behold, David seeketh thy hurt?

24:14 After whom is the king of Israel come out?

24:14 After whom dost thou pursue? after a dead dog, after a flea.

24:16 Is this thy voice, my son David?

24:19 For if a man find his enemy, will he let him go well away?

25:10 Who is David?

25:10 And who is the son of Jesse?

25:11 Shall I then take my bread, and my water, and my flesh that I have killed for my shearers, and give it unto men, whom I know not whence they be?

26:1 And the Ziphites came unto Saul to Gibeah, saying, Doth not David hide himself in the hill of Hachilah, which is before Jeshimon?

26:6 Who will go down with me to Saul to the camp? And Abishai said.

26:9 For who can stretch forth his hand against the LORD'S anointed, and be guiltless?

26:14 Answerest thou not, Abner?

26:14 Who art thou that criest to the king?

26:15 Art not thou a valiant man?

26:15 And who is like to thee in Israel?

26:15 Wherefore then hast thou not kept thy lord the king?

26:17 Is this thy voice, my son David?

26:18 Wherefore doth my lord thus pursue after his servant?

26:18 For what have I done?

26:18 What evil is in mine hand?

27:5 For why should thy servant dwell in the royal city with thee?

27:10 Whither have ye made a road to day?

28:9 Wherefore then layest thou a snare for my life, to cause me to die?

28:11 Whom shall I bring up unto thee?

28:12 Why hast thou deceived me?

28:13 Be not afraid: for what sawest thou?

28:14 What form is he of?

28:15 Why hast thou disquieted me, to bring me up?

28:16 Wherefore then dost thou ask of me, seeing the LORD is departed from thee, and is become thine enemy?

29:3 What do these Hebrews here?

29:3 Is not this David, the servant of Saul the king of Israel, which hath been with me these days, or these years, and I have found no fault in him since he fell unto me unto this day?

29:4 Wherewith should he reconcile himself unto his master?

29:4 Should it not be with the heads of these men?

29:5 Is not this David, of whom they sang one to another in dances, saying, Saul slew his thousands, and David his ten thousands?

29:8 But what have I done?

29:8 And what hast thou found in thy servant so long as I have been with thee unto this day, that I may not go fight against the enemies of my lord the king?

30:8 Shall I pursue after this troop?

30:8 Shall I overtake them?

30:13 To whom belongest thou?

30:13 And whence art thou?

30:15 Canst thou bring me down to this company?

30:24 For who will hearken unto you in this matter?

The Second Book of
Samuel—Otherwise Called the
Second Book of the Kings

1:3 From whence comest thou?

1:4 How went the matter?

1:5 How knowest thou that Saul and Jonathan his son be dead?

1:8 Who art thou?

1:13 Whence art thou?

1:14 How wast thou not afraid to stretch forth thine hand to destroy the LORD'S anointed?

2:1 Shall I go up into any of the cities of Judah?

2:1 Whither shall I go up?

2:20 Art thou Asahel?

2:22 Wherefore should I smite thee to the ground?

2:22 How then should I hold up my face to Joab thy brother?

2:26 Shall the sword devour for ever?

2:26 Knowest thou not that it will be bitterness in the latter end?

2:26 How long shall it be then, ere thou bid the people return from following their brethren?

3:7 Wherefore hast thou gone in unto my father's concubine?

3:8 Am I a dog's head, which against Judah do shew kindness this day unto the house of Saul thy father, to his brethren, and to his friends, and have not delivered thee into the hand of David, that thou chargest me to day with a fault concerning this woman?

3:12 Whose is the land?

3:24 What hast thou done?

3:24 Why is it that thou hast sent him away, and he is quite gone?

3:33 Died Abner as a fool dieth?

3:38 Know ye not that there is a prince and a great man fallen this day in Israel?

4:11 How much more, when wicked men have slain a righteous person in his own house upon his bed?

4:11 Shall I not therefore now require his blood of your hand, and take you away from the earth?

4:11 How much more, when wicked men have slain a righteous person in his own house upon his bed?

4:11 Shall I not therefore now require his blood of your hand, and take you away from the earth?

5:19 Shall I go up to the Philistines?

5:19 Wilt thou deliver them into mine hand?

6:9 How shall the ark of the LORD come to me?

7:5 Shalt thou build me an house for me to dwell in?

7:7 Why build ye not me an house of cedar?

7:18 Who am I, O Lord GOD?

7:18 And what is my house, that thou hast brought me hitherto?

7:19 Is this the manner of man, O Lord GOD?

7:20 And what can David say more unto thee?

7:23 What one nation in the earth is like thy people, even like Israel, whom God went to redeem for a people to himself, and to make him a name, and to do for you great things and terrible, for thy land, before thy people, which thou redeemedst to thee from Egypt, from the nations and their gods?

9:1 Is there yet any that is left of the house of Saul, that I may shew him kindness for Jonathan's sake?

9:2 Art thou Ziba?

9:3 Is there not yet any of the house of Saul, that I may shew the kindness of God unto him?

9:4 Where is he?

9:8 What is thy servant, that thou shouldest look upon such a dead dog as I am?

10:3 Thinkest thou that David doth honour thy father, that he hath sent comforters unto thee?

10:3 Hath not David rather sent his servants unto thee, to search the city, and to spy it out, and to overthrow it?

11:3 Is not this Bathsheba, the daughter of Eliam, the wife of Uriah the Hittite?

11:10 Camest thou not from thy journey?

11:10 Why then didst thou not go down unto thine house?

11:11 Shall I then go into mine house, to eat and to drink, and to lie with my wife?

11:20 Wherefore approached ye so nigh unto the city when ye did fight?

11:20 Knew ye not that they would shoot from the wall?

11:21 Who smote Abimelech the son of Jerubbesheth?

11:21 Did not a woman cast a piece of a millstone upon him from the wall, that he died in Thebez?

11:21 Why went ye nigh the wall?

12:9 Wherefore hast thou despised the commandment of the LORD, to do evil in his sight?

12:18 How will he then vex himself, if we tell him that the child is dead?

12:19 Is the child dead?

12:21 What thing is this that thou hast done?

12:22 Who can tell whether GOD will be gracious to me, that the child may live?

12:23 But now he is dead, wherefore should I fast?

12:23 Can I bring him back again?

13:4 Why art thou, being the king's son, lean from day to day?

13:4 Wilt thou not tell me?

13:13 Whither shall I cause my shame to go?

13:20 Hath Amnon thy brother been with thee?

13:26 Why should he go with thee?

13:28 Fear not: have not I commanded you? be courageous, and be valiant.

14:5 What aileth thee?

14:13 Wherefore then hast thou thought such a thing against the people of God?

14:19 Is not the hand of Joab with thee in all this?

14:31 Wherefore have thy servants set my field on fire?

14:32 Wherefore am I come from Geshur?

15:2 Of what city art thou?

15:19 Wherefore goest thou also with us?

15:20 Whereas thou camest but yesterday, should I this day make thee go up and down with us?

15:27 Art not thou a seer?

16:2 What meanest thou by these?

16:3 And where is thy master's son?

16:9 Why should this dead dog curse my lord the king?

16:10 What have I to do with you, ye sons of Zeruiah?

16:10 Who shall then say, Wherefore hast thou done so?

16:11 How much more now may this Benjamite do it?

16:17 Is this thy kindness to thy friend?

16:17 Why wentest thou not with thy friend?

16:19 Whom should I serve?

16:19 Should I not serve in the presence of his son?

17:6 Shall we do after his saying?

17:20 Where is Ahimaaz and Jonathan?

18:11 Why didst thou not smite him there to the ground?

18:22 Wherefore wilt thou run, my son, seeing that thou hast no tidings ready?

18:29 Is the young man Absalom safe?

18:32 Is the young man Absalom safe?

19:10 Why speak ye not a word of bringing the king back?

19:11 Why are ye the last to bring the king back to his house?

19:12 Ye are my brethren, ye are my bones and my flesh: wherefore then are ye the last to bring back the king?

19:13 Art thou not of my bone, and of my flesh?

19:21 Shall not Shimei be put to death for this, because he cursed the LORD'S anointed?

19:22 What have I to do with you, ye sons of Zeruiah, that ye should this day be adversaries unto me?

19:22 Shall there any man be put to death this day in Israel?

19:22 For do not I know that I am this day king over Israel?

19:25 Wherefore wentest not thou with me, Mephibosheth?

19:28 What right therefore have I yet to cry any more unto the king?

19:29 Why speakest thou any more of thy matters?

19:34 How long have I to live, that I should go up with the king unto Jerusalem?

19:35 I am this day fourscore years old: and can I discern between good and evil?

19:35 Can thy servant taste what I eat or what I drink?

19:35 Can I hear any more the voice of singing men and singing women?

19:35 Wherefore then should thy servant be yet a burden unto my lord the king?

19:36 Why should the king recompense it me with such a reward?

19:41 Why have our brethren the men of Judah stolen thee away, and have brought the king, and his household, and all David's men with him, over Jordan?

19:42 Because the king is near of kin to us: wherefore then be ye angry for this matter?

19:42 Have we eaten at all of the king's cost?

19:42 Hath he given us any gift?

19:43 Why then did ye despise us, that our advice should not be first had in bringing back our king?

20:9 Art thou in health, my brother?

20:17 Art thou Joab?

20:19 Why wilt thou swallow up the inheritance of the LORD?

21:3 What shall I do for you?

21:3 Wherewith shall I make the atonement, that ye may bless the inheritance of the LORD?

22:32 For who is God, save the LORD?

22:32 Who is a rock, save our God?

23:17 Is not this the blood of the men that went in jeopardy of their lives?

23:19 Was he not most honourable of three?

24:3 Why doth my lord the king delight in this thing?

24:13 Shall seven years of famine come unto thee in thy land?

24:13 Wilt thou flee three months before thine enemies, while they pursue thee?

24:13 Or that there be three days' pestilence in thy land?

24:17 What have they done?

24:21 Wherefore is my lord the king come to his servant?

The First Book of the
Kings—Commonly Called the
Third Book of the Kings

1:6 Why hast thou done so?

1:11 Hast thou not heard that Adonijah the son of Haggith doth reign, and David our lord knoweth it not?

1:13 Didst not thou, my lord, O king, swear unto thine handmaid, saying Assuredly Solomon thy son shall reign after me, and he shall sit upon my throne?

1:13 Why then doth Adonijah reign?

1:16 What wouldest thou?

1:24 Hast thou said, Adonijah shall reign after me, and he shall sit upon my throne?

1:27 Is this thing done by my lord the king, and thou hast not shewed it unto thy servant, who should sit on the throne of my lord the king after him?

1:41 Wherefore is this noise of the city being in an uproar?

2:13 Comest thou peaceably?

2:22 Why dost thou ask Abishag the Shunammite for Adonijah?

2:42 Did I not make thee to swear by the LORD, and protested unto thee, saying, Know for a certain, on the day thou goest out, and walkest abroad any whither, that thou shalt surely die?

2:43 Why then hast thou not kept the oath of the LORD, and the commandment that I have charged thee with?

3:9 Who is able to judge this thy so great a people?

8:27 But will God indeed dwell on the earth?

8:27 Behold, the heaven and heaven of heavens cannot contain thee; how much less this house that I have builded?

9:8 Why hath the LORD done thus unto this land, and to this house?

9:13 What cities are these which thou hast given me, my brother?

11:22 But what hast thou lacked with me, that, behold, thou seekest to go to thine own country?

11:41 And the rest of the acts of Solomon, and all that he did, and his wisdom, are they not written in the book of the acts of Solomon?

12:6 How do ye advise that I may answer this people?

12:9 What counsel give ye that we may answer this people, who have spoken to me, saying, Make the yoke which thy father did put upon us lighter?

12:16 What portion have we in David?

14:6 Why feignest thou thyself to be another?

14:29 Now the rest of the acts of Rehoboam, and all that he did, are they not written in the book of the chronicles of the kings of Judah?

15:7 Now the rest of the acts of Abijam, and all that he did, are they not written in the book of the chronicles of the kings of Judah?

15:23 The rest of all the acts of Asa, and all his might, and all that he did, and the cities which he built, are they not written in the book of the chronicles of the kings of Judah?

15:31 Now the rest of the acts of Nadab, and all that he did, are they not written in the book of the chronicles of the kings of Israel?

16:5 Now the rest of the acts of Baasha, and what he did, and his might, are they not written in the book of the chronicles of the kings of Israel?

16:14 Now the rest of the acts of Elah, and all that he did, are they not written in the book of the chronicles of the kings of Israel?

16:20 Now the rest of the acts of Zimri, and his treason that he wrought, are they not written in the book of the chronicles of the kings of Israel?

16:27 Now the rest of the acts of Omri which he did, and his might that he shewed, are they not written in the book of the chronicles of the kings of Israel?

17:18 What have I to do with thee, O thou man of God?

17:18 Art thou come unto me to call my sin to remembrance, and to slay my son?

17:20 And he cried unto the LORD, and said, O LORD my God, hast thou also brought evil upon the widow with whom I sojourn, by slaying her son?

18:7 Art thou that my lord Elijah?

18:9 What have I sinned, that thou wouldest deliver thy servant into the hand of Ahab, to slay me?

18:13 Was it not told my lord what I did when Jezebel slew the prophets of the LORD, how I hid an hundred men of the LORD'S prophets by fifty in a cave, and fed them with bread and water?

18:17 Art thou he that troubleth Israel?

18:21 How long halt ye between two opinions?

19:9 What doest thou here, Elijah?

19:13 What doest thou here, Elijah?

19:20 What have I done to thee?

20:13 Hast thou seen all this great multitude?

20:14 By whom?

20:14 Who shall order the battle?

20:32 Is he yet alive?

21:5 Why is thy spirit so sad, that thou eatest no bread?

21:7 Dost thou now govern the kingdom of Israel?

21:19 Thus saith the LORD, Hast thou killed, and also taken possession?

21:20 Hast thou found me, O mine enemy?

21:29 Seest thou how Ahab humbleth himself before me?

22:3 Know ye that Ramoth in Gilead is ours, and we be still, and take it not out of the hand of the king of Syria?

22:4 Wilt thou go with me to battle to Ramothgilead?

22:6 Shall I go against Ramothgilead to battle, or shall I forbear?

22:7 Is there not here a prophet of the LORD besides, that we might enquire of him?

22:15 Shall we go against Ramothgilead to battle, or shall we forbear?

22:16 How many times shall I adjure thee that thou tell me nothing but that which is true in the name of the LORD?

22:18 Did I not tell thee that he would prophesy no good concerning me, but evil?

22:20 Who shall persuade Ahab, that he may go up and fall at Ramothgilead?

22:22 Wherewith?

22:24 Which way went the Spirit of the LORD from me to speak unto thee?

22:39 Now the rest of the acts of Ahab, and all that he did, and the ivory house which he made, and all the cities that he built, are they not written in the book of the chronicles of the kings of Israel?

22:45 Now the rest of the acts of Jehoshaphat, and his might that he shewed, and how he warred, are they not written in the book of the chronicles of the kings of Judah?

The Second Book of the
Kings—Commonly Called the
Fourth Book of the Kings

1:3 Is it not because there is not a God in Israel, that ye go to enquire of Baalzebub the god of Ekron?

1:5 Why are ye now turned back?

1:6 Thus saith the LORD, Is it not because there is not a God in Israel, that thou sendest to enquire of Baalzebub the god of Ekron?

1:7 What manner of man was he which came up to meet you, and told you these words?

1:18 Now the rest of the acts of Ahaziah which he did, are they not written in the book of the chronicles of the kings of Israel?

2:3 Knowest thou that the LORD will take away thy master from thy head to day?

2:5 Knowest thou that the LORD will take away thy master from thy head to day?

2:14 And he took the mantle of Elijah that fell from him, and smote the waters, and said, Where is the LORD God of Elijah? and when he also had smitten the waters, they parted hither and thither: and Elisha went over.

2:18 Did I not say unto you, Go not?

3:7 Wilt thou go with me against Moab to battle?

3:8 Which way shall we go up?

3:11 Is there not here a prophet of the LORD, that we may enquire of the LORD by him?

3:13 What have I to do with thee?

4:2 What shall I do for thee?

4:2 Tell me, what hast thou in the house?

4:13 What is to be done for thee?

4:13 Wouldest thou be spoken for to the king, or to the captain of the host?

4:14 What then is to be done for her?

4:23 Wherefore wilt thou go to him to day?

4:26 Is it well with thee?

4:26 Is it well with thy husband?

4:26 Is it well with the child?

4:28 Did I desire a son of my lord?

4:28 Did I not say, Do not deceive me?

4:43 What, should I set this before an hundred men?

5:7 Am I God, to kill and to make alive, that this man doth send unto me to recover a man of his leprosy?

5:8 Wherefore hast thou rent thy clothes?

5:12 Are not Abana and Pharpar, rivers of Damascus, better than all the waters of Israel?

5:12 May I not wash in them, and be clean? So he turned and went away in a rage.

5:13 My father, if the prophet had bid thee do some great thing, wouldest thou not have done it?

5:13 How much rather then, when he saith to thee, Wash, and be clean?

5:17 Shall there not then, I pray thee, be given to thy servant two mules' burden of earth?

5:21 Is all well?

5:25 Whence comest thou, Gehazi?

5:26 Went not mine heart with thee, when the man turned again from his chariot to meet thee?

5:26 Is it a time to receive money, and to receive garments, and oliveyards, and vineyards, and sheep, and oxen, and menservants, and maidservants?

6:6 Where fell it?

6:11 Will ye not shew me which of us is for the king of Israel?

6:15 Alas, my master! how shall we do?

6:21 My father, shall I smite them?

6:21 Shall I smite them?

6:22 Wouldest thou smite those whom thou hast taken captive with thy sword and with thy bow?

6:27 If the LORD do not help thee, whence shall I help thee?

6:27 Out of the barnfloor, or out of the winepress?

6:28 What aileth thee?

6:32 See ye how this son of a murderer hath sent to take away mine head?

6:32 Is not the sound of his master's feet behind him?

6:33 What should I wait for the LORD any longer?

7:2 Behold, if the LORD would make windows in heaven, might this thing be?

7:3 Why sit we here until we die?

7:19 If the LORD should make windows in heaven, might such a thing be?

8:8 Shall I recover of this disease?

8:9 Thy son Benhadad king of Syria hath sent me to thee, saying, Shall I recover of this disease?

8:12 Why weepeth my lord?

8:13 But what, is thy servant a dog, that he should do this great thing?

8:14 What said Elisha to thee?

8:23 And the rest of the acts of Joram, and all that he did, are they not written in the book of the chronicles of the kings of Judah?

9:5 Unto which of all us?

9:11 Is all well?

9:11 Wherefore came this mad fellow to thee?

9:17 Is it peace?

9:18 Thus saith the king, Is it peace?

9:18 What hast thou to do with peace?

9:19 Thus saith the king, Is it peace?

9:19 What hast thou to do with peace?

9:22 Is it peace, Jehu?

9:22 What peace, so long as the whoredoms of thy mother Jezebel and her witchcrafts are so many?

9:31 Had Zimri peace, who slew his master?

9:32 Who is on my side?

9:32 Who?

10:4 Behold, two kings stood not before him: how then shall we stand?

10:9 Ye be righteous: behold, I conspired against my master, and slew him: but who slew all these?

10:13 Who are ye?

10:15 Is thine heart right, as my heart is with thy heart?

10:34 Now the rest of the acts of Jehu, and all that he did, and all his might, are they not written in the book of the chronicles of the kings of Israel?

12:7 Why repair ye not the breaches of the house?

12:19 And the rest of the acts of Joash, and all that he did, are they not written in the book of the chronicles of the kings of Judah?

13:8 Now the rest of the acts of Jehoahaz, and all that he did, and his might, are they not written in the book of the chronicles of the kings of Israel?

13:12 And the rest of the acts of Joash, and all that he did, and his might wherewith he fought against Amaziah king of Judah, are they not written in the book of the chronicles of the kings of Israel?

14:10 Why shouldest thou meddle to thy hurt, that thou shouldest fall, even thou, and Judah with thee?

14:15 Now the rest of the acts of Jehoash which he did, and his might, and how he fought with Amaziah king of Judah, are they not written in the book of the chronicles of the kings of Israel?

14:18 And the rest of the acts of Amaziah, are they not written in the book of the chronicles of the kings of Judah?

14:28 And the rest of the acts of Amaziah, are they not written in the book of the chronicles of the kings of Judah?

15:6 And the rest of the acts of Azariah, and all that he did, are they not written in the book of the chronicles of the kings of Judah?

15:21 And the rest of the acts of Menahem, and all that he did, are they not written in the book of the chronicles of the kings of Israel?

15:36 Now the rest of the acts of Jotham, and all that he did, are they not written in the book of the chronicles of the kings of Judah?

16:19 Now the rest of the acts of Ahaz which he did, are they not written in the book of the chronicles of the kings of Judah?

18:19 What confidence is this wherein thou trustest?

18:20 Now on whom dost thou trust, that thou rebellest against me?

18:22 But if ye say unto me, We trust in the LORD our God: is not that he, whose high places and whose altars Hezekiah hath taken away, and hath said to Judah and Jerusalem, Ye shall worship before this altar in Jerusalem?

18:24 How then wilt thou turn away the face of one captain of the least of my master's servants, and put thy trust on Egypt for chariots and for horsemen?

18:25 Am I now come up without the LORD against this place to destroy it?

18:27 Hath my master sent me to thy master, and to thee, to speak these words?

18:27 Hath he not sent me to the men which sit on the wall, that they may eat their own dung, and drink their own piss with you?

18:33 Hath any of the gods of the nations delivered at all his land out of the hand of the king of Assyria?

18:34 Where are the gods of Hamath, and of Arpad?

18:34 Where are the gods of Sepharvaim, Hena, and Ivah?

18:34 Have they delivered Samaria out of mine hand?

18:35 Who are they among all the gods of the countries, that have delivered their country out of mine hand, that the LORD should deliver Jerusalem out of mine hand?

19:11 Shalt thou be delivered?

19:12 Have the gods of the nations delivered them which my fathers have destroyed; as Gozan, and Haran, and Rezeph, and the children of Eden which were in Thelasar?

19:13 Where is the king of Hamath, and the king of Arpad, and the king of the city of Sepharvaim, of Hena, and Ivah?

19:22 Whom hast thou reproached and blasphemed?

19:22 Against whom hast thou exalted thy voice, and lifted up thine eyes on high?

19:25 Hast thou not heard long ago how I have done it, and of ancient times that I have formed it?

20:8 What shall be the sign that the LORD will heal me, and that I shall go up into the house of the LORD the third day?

20:9 Shall the shadow go forward ten degrees, or go back ten degrees?

20:14 What said these men?

20:14 From whence came they unto thee?

20:15 What have they seen in thine house?

20:19 Is it not good, if peace and truth be in my days?

20:20 And the rest of the acts of Hezekiah, and all his might, and how he made a pool, and a conduit, and brought water into the city, are they not written in the book of the chronicles of the kings of Judah?

21:17 Now the rest of the acts of Manasseh, and all that he did, and his sin that he sinned, are they not written in the book of the chronicles of the kings of Judah?

21:25 Now the rest of the acts of Amon which he did, are they not written in the book of the chronicles of the kings of Judah?

23:17 What title is that that I see?

23:28 Now the rest of the acts of Josiah, and all that he did, are they not written in the book of the chronicles of the kings of Judah?

24:5 Now the rest of the acts of Jehoiakim, and all that he did, are they not written in the book of the chronicles of the kings of Judah?

The First Book of the
Chronicles

11:19 Shall I drink the blood of these men that have put their lives in jeopardy?

13:12 How shall I bring the ark of God home to me?

14:10 Shall I go up against the Philistines?

14:10 And wilt thou deliver them into mine hand?

17:6 Wheresoever I have walked with all Israel, spake I a word to any of the judges of Israel, whom I commanded to feed my people, saying, Why have ye not built me an house of cedars?

17:16 Who am I, O LORD God, and what is mine house, that thou hast brought me hitherto?

17:18 What can David speak more to thee for the honour of thy servant?

17:21 What one nation in the earth is like thy people Israel, whom God went to redeem to be his own people, to make thee a name of greatness and terribleness, by driving out nations from before thy people, whom thou hast redeemed out of Egypt?

19:3 Thinkest thou that David doth honour thy father, that he hath sent comforters unto thee?

19:3 Are not his servants come unto thee for to search, and to overthrow, and to spy out the land?

21:3 My lord the king, are they not all my lord's servants?

21:3 Why then doth my lord require this thing?

21:3 Why will he be a cause of trespass to Israel?

21:17 Is it not I that commanded the people to be numbered?

21:17 Even I it is that have sinned and done evil indeed; but as for these sheep, what have they done?

22:18 Is not the LORD your God with you?

22:18 Hath he not given you rest on every side?

29:5 Who then is willing to consecrate his service this day unto the LORD?

29:14 But who am I, and what is my people, that we should be able to offer so willingly after this sort? for all things come of thee, and of thine own have we given thee.

The Second Book of the
Chronicles

1:10 Who can judge this thy people, that is so great?

2:6 Who is able to build him an house, seeing the heaven and heaven of heavens cannot contain him?

2:6 Who am I then, that I should build him an house, save only to burn sacrifice before him?

6:18 But will God in very deed dwell with men on the earth?

7:21 And this house, which is high, shall be an astonishment to every one that passeth by it; so that he shall say, Why hath the LORD done thus unto this land, and unto this house?

9:29 Now the rest of the acts of Solomon, first and last, are they not written in the book of Nathan the prophet, and in the prophecy of Ahijah the Shilonite, and in the visions of Iddo the seer against Jeroboam the son of Nebat?

10:6 What counsel give ye me to return answer to this people?

10:9 What advice give ye that we may return answer to this people, which have spoken to me, saying Ease somewhat the yoke that thy father did put upon us?

10:16 What portion have we in David?

12:15 Now the acts of Rehoboam, first and last, are they not written in the book of Shemaiah the prophet, and of Iddo the seer concerning genealogies? And there were wars between Rehoboam and Jeroboam continually.

13:5 Ought ye not to know that the LORD God of Israel gave the kingdom over Israel to David for ever, even to him and to his sons by a covenant of salt?

13:9 Have ye not cast out the priests of the LORD, the sons of Aaron, and the Levites, and have made you priests after the manner of the nations of other lands?

16:8 Were not the Ethiopians and the Lubims a huge host, with very many chariots and horsemen?

18:3 Wilt thou go with me to Ramothgilead?

18:5 Shall we go to Ramothgilead to battle, or shall I forbear?

18:6 Is there not here a prophet of the LORD besides, that we might enquire of him?

18:14 Shall we go to Ramothgilead to battle, or shall I forbear?

18:15 How many times shall I adjure thee that thou say nothing but the truth to me in the name of the LORD?

18:17 Did I not tell thee that he would not prophesy good unto me, but evil?

18:19 Who shall entice Ahab king of Israel, that he may go up and fall at Ramothgilead?

18:20 Then there came out a spirit, and stood before the LORD, and said, I will entice him. And the LORD said unto him, Wherewith?

18:23 Which way went the Spirit of the LORD from me to speak unto thee?

19:2 Shouldest thou help the ungodly, and love them that hate the LORD?

20:6 O LORD God of our fathers, art not thou God in heaven?

20:6 Rulest not thou over all the kingdoms of the heathen?

20:6 In thine hand is there not power and might, so that none is able to withstand thee?

20:7 Art not thou our God, who didst drive out the inhabitants of this land before thy people Israel, and gavest it to the seed of Abraham thy friend for ever?

20:12 Wilt thou not judge them?

24:6 Why hast thou not required of the Levites to bring in out of Judah and out of Jerusalem the collection, according to the commandment of Moses the servant of the LORD, and of the congregation of Israel, for the tabernacle of witness?

24:20 Why transgress ye the commandments of the LORD, that ye cannot prosper?

25:9 What shall we do for the hundred talents which I have given to the army of Israel?

25:15 Why hast thou sought after the gods of the people, which could not deliver their own people out of thine hand?

25:16 Art thou made of the king's counsel?

25:16 Why shouldest thou be smitten?

25:19 Why shouldest thou meddle to thine hurt, that thou shouldest fall, even thou, and Judah with thee?

25:26 Now the rest of the acts of Amaziah, first and last, behold, are they not written in the book of the kings of Judah and Israel?

28:10 Are there not with you, even with you, sins against the LORD your God?

32:4 Why should the kings of Assyria come, and find much water?

32:10 Whereon do ye trust, that ye abide in the siege in Jerusalem?

32:11 Doth not Hezekiah persuade you to give over yourselves to die by famine and by thirst, saying, The LORD our God shall deliver us out of the hand of the king of Assyria?

32:12 Hath not the same Hezekiah taken away his high places and his altars, and commanded Judah and Jerusalem, saying, Ye shall worship before one altar, and burn incense upon it?

32:13 Know ye not what I and my fathers have done unto all the people of other lands?

32:13 Were the gods of the nations of those lands any ways able to deliver their lands out of mine hand?

32:14 Who was there among all the gods of those nations that my fathers utterly destroyed, that could deliver his people out of mine hand, that your God should be able to deliver you out of mine hand?

32:15 Now therefore let not Hezekiah deceive you, nor persuade you on this manner, neither yet believe him: for no god of any nation or kingdom was able to deliver his people out of mine hand, and out of the hand of my fathers: how much less shall your God deliver you out of mine hand?

35:21 What have I to do with thee, thou king of Judah?

36:23 Who is there among you of all his people?

The Book of
Ezra

1:3 Who is there among you of all his people?

4:22 Why should damage grow to the hurt of the kings?

5:3 Who hath commanded you to build this house, and to make up this wall?

5:4 What are the names of the men that make this building?

5:9 Who commanded you to build this house, and to make up these walls?

7:23 Whatsoever is commanded by the God of heaven, let it be diligently done for the house of the God of heaven: for why should there be wrath against the realm of the king and his sons?

9:14 Should we again break thy commandments, and join in affinity with the people of these abominations?

9:14 Wouldest not thou be angry with us till thou hadst consumed us, so that there should be no remnant nor escaping?

The Book of
Nehemiah

2:2 Why is thy countenance sad, seeing thou art not sick?

2:3 Why should not my countenance be sad, when the city, the place of my fathers' sepulchres, lieth waste, and the gates thereof are consumed with fire?

2:4 For what dost thou make request?

2:6 For how long shall thy journey be?

2:6 When wilt thou return?

2:19 What is this thing that ye do?

2:19 Will ye rebel against the king?

4:2 What do these feeble Jews?

4:2 Will they fortify themselves?

4:2 Will they sacrifice?

4:2 Will they make an end in a day?

4:2 Will they revive the stones out of the heaps of the rubbish which are burned?

5:8 Will ye even sell your brethren?

5:8 Shall they be sold unto us?

5:9 Ought ye not to walk in the fear of our God because of the reproach of the heathen our enemies?

8:6 How can I endure to see the destruction of my kindred?

9:12 What have they done in the rest of the king's provinces?

9:12 Now what is thy petition?

9:12 What is thy request further?

10:2 And all the acts of his power and of his might, and the declaration of the greatness of Mordecai, whereunto the king advanced him, are they not written in the book of the chronicles of the kings of Media and Persia?

*Who knoweth whether thou art come to the
kingdom for such a time as this?*
Esther 4:14

POETRY

Is not my help in me?
Job 6:13

The Book of
Job

1:7 Whence comest thou?

1:8 Hast thou considered my servant Job, that there is none like him in the earth, a perfect and an upright man, one that feareth God, and escheweth evil?

1:9 Doth Job fear God for nought?

1:10 Hast not thou made an hedge about him, and about his house, and about all that he hath on every side?

2:2 From whence comest thou?

2:3 Hast thou considered my servant Job, that there is none like him in the earth, a perfect and an upright man, one that feareth God, and escheweth evil?

2:9 Dost thou still retain thine integrity?

2:10 What?

2:10 Shall we receive good at the hand of God, and shall we not receive evil?

3:11 Why died I not from the womb?

3:11 Why did I not give up the ghost when I came out of the belly?

3:12 Why did the knees prevent me?

3:12 Why the breasts that I should suck?

3:20, 21, 22 Wherefore is light given to him that is in misery, and life unto the bitter in soul; Which long for death, but it cometh not; and dig for it more than for hid treasures; Which rejoice exceedingly, and are glad, when they can find the grave?

3:23 Why is light given to a man whose way is hid, and whom God hath hedged in?

4:2 If we assay to commune with thee, wilt thou be grieved?

4:2 But who can withhold himself from speaking?

4:6 Is not this thy fear, thy confidence, thy hope, and the uprightness of thy ways?

4:7 Who ever perished, being innocent?

4:7 Where were the righteous cut off?

4:17 Shall mortal man be more just than God?

4:17 Shall a man be more pure than his maker?

4:19 How much less in them that dwell in houses of clay, whose foundation is in the dust, which are crushed before the moth?

5:1 Call now, if there be any that will answer thee; and to which of the saints wilt thou turn?

6:5 Doth the wild ass bray when he hath grass?

6:5 Or loweth the ox over his fodder?

6:6 Can that which is unsavoury be eaten without salt?

6:6 Is there any taste in the white of an egg?

6:11 What is my strength, that I should hope?

6:11 What is mine end, that I should prolong my life?

6:12 Is my strength the strength of stones?

6:12 Is my flesh of brass?

6:13 Is not my help in me?

6:13 Is wisdom driven quite from me?

6:22 Did I say, Bring unto me?

6:22 Or, Give a reward for me of your substance?

6:23 Or, Deliver me from the enemy's hand?

6:23 Or, Redeem me from the hand of the mighty?

6:25 How forcible are right words! but what doth your arguing reprove?

6:26 Do ye imagine to reprove words, and the speeches of one that is desperate, which are as wind?

6:30 Is there iniquity in my tongue?

6:30 Cannot my taste discern perverse things?

7:1 Is there not an appointed time to man upon earth?

7:1 Are not his days also like the days of an hireling?

7:4 When I lie down, I say, When shall I arise, and the night be gone?

7:12 Am I a sea, or a whale, that thou settest a watch over me?

7:17 What is man, that thou shouldest magnify him?

7:17 And that thou shouldest set thine heart upon him?

7:18 And that thou shouldest visit him every morning, and try him every moment?

7:19 How long wilt thou not depart from me, nor let me alone till I swallow down my spittle?

7:20 What shall I do unto thee, O thou preserver of men?

7:20 Why hast thou set me as a mark against thee, so that I am a burden to myself?

7:21 Why dost thou not pardon my transgression, and take away mine iniquity?

8:2 How long wilt thou speak these things?

8:2 How long shall the words of thy mouth be like a strong wind?

8:3 Doth God pervert judgment?

8:3 Doth the Almighty pervert justice?

8:10 Shall not they teach thee, and tell thee, and utter words out of their heart?

8:11 Can the rush grow up without mire?

8:11 Can the flag grow without water?

9:2 How should man be just with God?

9:4 Who hath hardened himself against him, and hath prospered?

9:12 Who can hinder him?

9:12 Who will say unto him, What doest thou?

9:14 How much less shall I answer him, and choose out my words to reason with him?

9:19 Who shall set me a time to plead?

9:24 Where, and who is he?

9:29 If I be wicked, why then labour I in vain?

10:3 Is it good unto thee that thou shouldest oppress, that thou shouldest despise the work of thine hands, and shine upon the counsel of the wicked?

10:4 Hast thou eyes of flesh?

10:4 Seest thou as man seeth?

10:5 Are thy days as the days of man?

10:5, 6 Are thy years as man's days, that thou enquirest after mine iniquity, and searchest after my sin?

10:9 Wilt thou bring me into dust again?

10:10 Hast thou not poured me out as milk, and curdled me like cheese?

10:18 Wherefore then hast thou brought me forth out of the womb?

10:20 Are not my days few?

11:2 Should not the multitude of words be answered?

11:2 Should a man full of talk be justified?

11:3 Should thy lies make men hold their peace?

11:3 When thou mockest, shall no man make thee ashamed?

11:7 Canst thou by searching find out God?

11:8 What canst thou do?

11:8 What canst thou know?

11:10 If he cut off, and shut up, or gather together, then who can hinder him?

11:11 Will he not then consider it?

12:3 Who knoweth not such things as these?

12:9 Who knoweth not in all these that the hand of the LORD hath wrought this?

12:11 Doth not the ear try words?

12:11 And the mouth taste his meat?

13:7 Will ye speak wickedly for God?

13:7 And talk deceitfully for him?

13:8 Will ye accept his person?

13:8 Will ye contend for God?

13:9 Is it good that he should search you out?

13:9 As one man mocketh another, do ye so mock him?

13:11 Shall not his excellency make you afraid?

13:11 And his dread fall upon you?

13:14 Wherefore do I take my flesh in my teeth, and put my life in mine hand?

13:24 Wherefore hidest thou thy face, and holdest me for thine enemy?

13:25 Wilt thou break a leaf driven to and fro?

13:25 Wilt thou pursue the dry stubble?

14:3 Dost thou open thine eyes upon such an one, and bringest me into judgment with thee?

14:4 Who can bring a clean thing out of an unclean?

14:10 Where is he?

14:14 If a man die, shall he live again?

14:16 Dost thou not watch over my sin?

15:2 Should a wise man utter vain knowledge, and fill his belly with the east wind?

15:3 Should he reason with unprofitable talk?

15:3 Or with speeches wherewith he can do no good?

15:7 Art thou the first man that was born?

15:7 Wast thou made before the hills?

15:8 Hast thou heard the secret of God?

15:8 Dost thou restrain wisdom to thyself?

15:9 What knowest thou, that we know not?

15:9 What understandest thou, which is not in us?

15:11 Are the consolations of God small with thee?

15:11 Is there any secret thing with thee?

15:12 Why doth thine heart carry thee away?

15:12, 13 And what do thy eyes wink at, that thou turnest thou spirit against God, and lettest such words go out of thy mouth?

15:14 What is man, that he should be clean?

15:14 And he which is born of a woman, that he should be righteous?

15:16 How much more abominable and filthy is man, which drinketh iniquity like water?

15:23 Where is it?

16:3 Shall vain words have an end?

16:3 What emboldeneth thee that thou answerest?

16:6 What am I eased?

17:2 Are there not mockers with me?

17:2 Doth not mine eye continue in their provocation?

17:3 Who is he that will strike hands with me?

17:15 Where is now my hope?

17:15 Who shall see it?

18:2 How long will it be ere ye make an end of words?

18:3 Wherefore are we counted as beasts, and reputed vile in your sight?

18:4 He teareth himself in his anger: shall the earth be forsaken for thee?

18:4 Shall the rock be removed out of his place?

19:2 How long will ye vex my soul, and break me in pieces with words?

19:22 Why do ye persecute me as God, and are not satisfied with my flesh?

19:28 Why persecute we him, seeing the root of the matter is found in me?

20:4, 5 Knowest thou not this of old, since man was placed upon earth, That the triumphing of the wicked is short, and the joy of the hypocrite but for a moment?

20:7 Where is he?

21:4 Is my complaint to man?

21:4 Why should not my spirit be troubled?

21:7 Wherefore do the wicked live, become old, yea, are mighty in power?

21:15 What is the Almighty, that we should serve him?

21:15 What profit should we have, if we pray unto him?

21:21 What pleasure hath he in his house after him, when the number of his months is cut off in the midst?

21:22 Shall any teach God knowledge?

21:28 Where is the house of the prince?

21:28 Where are the dwelling places of the wicked?

21:29 Have ye not asked them that go by the way?

21:29,30 And do ye not know their tokens, that the wicked is reserved to the day of destruction? they shall be brought forth to the day of wrath.

21:31 Who shall declare his way to his face?

21:31 Who shall repay him what he hath done?

21:34 How then comfort ye me in vain, seeing in your answers there remaineth falsehood?

22:2 Can a man be profitable unto God, as he that is wise may be profitable unto himself?

22:3 Is it any pleasure to the Almighty, that thou art righteous?

22:3 Is it gain to him, that thou makest thy ways perfect?

22:4 Will he reprove thee for fear of thee?

22:4 Will he enter with thee into judgment?

22:5 Is not thy wickedness great?

22:5 And thine iniquities infinite?

22:12 Is not God in the height of heaven?

22:13 How doth God know?

22:13 Can he judge through the dark cloud?

22:15 Hast thou marked the old way which wicked men have trodden?

22:17 What can the Almighty do for them?

23:6 Will he plead against me with his great power?

24:1 Why, seeing times are not hidden from the Almighty, do they that know him not see his days?

24:25 Who will make me a liar, and make my speech nothing worth?

25:3 Is there any number of his armies?

25:3 Upon whom doth not his light arise?

25:4 How then can man be justified with God?

25:4 How can he be clean that is born of a woman?

25:6 How much less man, that is a worm?

25:6 And the son of man, which is a worm?

26:2 How hast thou helped him that is without power?

26:2 How savest thou the arm that hath no strength?

26:3 How hast thou counselled him that hath no wisdom?

26:3 How hast thou plentifully declared the thing as it is?

26:4 To whom hast thou uttered words?

26:4 Whose spirit came from thee?

26:14 How little a portion is heard of him?

26:14 Who can understand?

27:8 For what is the hope of the hypocrite, though he hath gained, when God taketh away his soul?

27:9 Will God hear his cry when trouble cometh upon him?

27:10 Will he delight himself in the Almighty?

27:10 Will he always call upon God?

27:12 Why then are ye thus altogether vain?

28:12 Where shall wisdom be found?

28:12 Where is the place of understanding?

28:20 Whence then cometh wisdom?

28:20 Where is the place of understanding?

30:2 Whereto might the strength of their hands profit me, in whom old age was perished?

30:25 Did not I weep for him that was in trouble?

30:25 Was not my soul grieved for the poor?

31:1 Why then should I think upon a maid?

31:2 What portion of God is there from above?

31:2 What inheritance of the Almighty from on high?

31:3 Is not destruction to the wicked?

31:3 And a strange punishment to the workers of iniquity?

31:4 Doth not he see my ways, and count all my steps?

31:14 What then shall I do when God riseth up?

31:14 When he visiteth, what shall I answer him?

31:15 Did not he that made me in the womb make him?

31:15 Did not one fashion us in the womb?

31:34 Did I fear a great multitude, or did the contempt of families terrify me, that I kept silence, and went not out of the door?

33:13 Why dost thou strive against him?

34:6 Should I lie against my right?

34:7 What man is like Job, who drinketh up scorning like water?

34:13 Who hath given him a charge over the earth?

34:13 Who hath disposed the whole world?

34:17 Shall even he that hateth right govern?

34:17 Wilt thou condemn him that is most just?

34:18 Is it fit to say to a king, Thou art wicked?

34:18 And to princes, Ye are ungodly?

34:19 How much less to him that accepteth not the persons of princes, nor regardeth the rich more than the poor?

34:29 When he giveth quietness, who then can make trouble?

34:29 When he hideth his face, who then can behold him?

34:33 Should it be according to thy mind?

35:2 Thinkest thou this to be right, that thou saidst, My righteousness is more than God's?

35:3 What advantage will it be unto thee?

35:3 What profit shall I have, if I be cleansed from my sin?

35:6 If thou sinnest, what doest thou against him?

35:6 If thy transgressions be multiplied, what doest thou unto him?

35:7 If thou be righteous, what givest thou him?

35:7 What receiveth he of thine hand?

35:10, 11 Where is God my maker, who giveth songs in the night; Who teacheth us more than the beasts of the earth, and maketh us wiser than the fowls of heaven?

36:19 Will he esteem thy riches?

36:22 Who teacheth like him?

36:23 Who hath enjoined him his way?

36:23 Who can say, Thou hast wrought iniquity?

36:29 Can any understand the spreadings of the clouds, or the noise of his tabernacle?

37:15 Dost thou know when God disposed them, and caused the light of his cloud to shine?

37:16 Dost thou know the balancings of the clouds, the wondrous works of him which is perfect in knowledge?

37:17 How thy garments are warm, when he quieteth the earth by the south wind?

37:18 Hast thou with him spread out the sky, which is strong, and as a molten looking glass?

37:20 Shall it be told him that I speak?

38:2 Who is this that darkeneth counsel by words without knowledge?

38:4 Where wast thou when I laid the foundations of the earth?

38:5 Who hath laid the measures thereof, if thou knowest?

38:5 Who hath stretched the line upon it?

38:6 Whereupon are the foundations thereof fastened?

38:6, 7 Or who laid the corner stone thereof; when the morning stars sang together, and all the sons of God shouted for joy?

38:8 Who shut up the sea with doors, when it brake forth, as if it had issued out of the womb?

38:9, 10, 11 When I made the cloud the garment thereof, and thick darkness a swaddlingband for it, And brake up for it my decreed place, and set bars and doors, And said hitherto shalt thou come, but no further: and here shall thy proud waves be stayed?

38:12, 13 Hast thou commanded the morning since thy days and caused the dayspring to know his place; that it might take hold of the ends of the earth, that the wicked might be shaken out of it?

38:16 Hast thou entered into the springs of the sea?

38:16 Hast thou walked in the search of the depth?

38:17 Have the gates of death been opened unto thee?

38:17 Hast thou seen the doors of the shadow of death?

38:18 Hast thou perceived the breadth of the earth?

38:19 Where is the way where light dwelleth?

38:19, 20 And as for darkness, where is the place thereof, that thou shouldest take it to the bound thereof, and that thou shouldest know the paths to the house thereof?

38:21 Knowest thou it, because thou wast then born?

38:21 Or because the number of thy days is great?

38:22 Hast thou entered into the treasures of the snow?

38:22, 23 Hast thou seen the treasures of the hail, which I reserved against the time of trouble, against the day of battle and war?

38:24 By what way is the light parted, which scattereth the east wind upon the earth?

38:25, 26, 27 Who hath divided a watercourse for the overflowing of waters, or a way for the lightning of thunder; to cause it to rain on the earth, where no man is; on the wilderness, wherein there is no man; to satisfy the desolate and waste ground; and to cause the bud of the tender herb to spring forth?

38:28 Hath the rain a father?

38:28 Who hath begotten the drops of dew?

38:29 Out of whose womb came the ice?

38:29 The hoary frost of heaven, who hath gendered it?

38:31 Canst thou bind the sweet influences of Pleiades, or loose the bands of Orion?

38:32 Canst thou bring forth Mazzaroth in his season?

38:32 Canst thou guide Arcturus with his sons?

38:33 Knowest thou the ordinances of heaven?

38:33 Canst thou set the dominion thereof in the earth?

38:34 Canst thou lift up thy voice to the clouds, that abundance of waters may cover thee?

38:35 Canst thou send lightnings, that they may go, and say unto thee, Here we are?

38:36 Who hath put wisdom in the inward parts?

38:36 Who hath given understanding to the heart?

38:37 Who can number the clouds in wisdom?

38:37, 38 Or who can stay the bottles of heaven, when the dust groweth into hardness, and the clods cleave fast together?

38:39 Wilt thou hunt the prey for the lion?

38:39, 40 Or fill the appetite of the young lions, when they couch in their dens, and abide in the covert to lie in wait?

38:41 Who provideth for the raven his food? when his young ones cry unto God, they wander for lack of meat.

39:1 Knowest thou the time when the wild goats of the rock bring forth?

39:1 Canst thou mark when the hinds do calve?

39:2 Canst thou number the months that they fulfil?

39:2 Knowest thou the time when they bring forth?

39:5 Who hath sent out the wild ass free?

39:5 Who hath loosed the bands of the wild ass?

39:9 Will the unicorn be willing to serve thee, or abide by thy crib?

39:10 Canst thou bind the unicorn with his band in the furrow?

39:10 Will he harrow the valleys after thee?

39:11 Wilt thou trust him, because his strength is great?

39:11 Wilt thou leave thy labour to him?

39:12 Wilt thou believe him, that he will bring home thy seed, and gather it into thy barn?

39:13 Gavest thou the goodly wings unto the peacocks?

39:13 Or wings and feathers unto the ostrich?

39:19 Hast thou given the horse strength?

39:19 Hast thou clothed his neck with thunder?

39:20 Canst thou make him afraid as a grasshopper?

39:26 Doth the hawk fly by thy wisdom, and stretch her wings toward the south?

39:27 Doth the eagle mount up at thy command, and make her nest on high?

40:2 Shall he that contendeth with the Almighty instruct him?

40:4 Behold, I am vile; what shall I answer thee?

40:8 Wilt thou also disannul my judgment?

40:8 Wilt thou condemn me, that thou mayest be righteous?

40:9 Hast thou an arm like God?

40:9 Canst thou thunder with a voice like him?

41:1 Canst thou draw out leviathan with an hook?

41:1 Or his tongue with a cord which thou lettest down?

41:2 Canst thou put an hook into his nose?

41:2 Or bore his jaw through with a thorn?

41:3 Will he make many supplications unto thee?

41:3 Will he speak soft words unto thee?

41:4 Will he make a covenant with thee?

41:4 Wilt thou take him for a servant for ever?

41:5 Wilt thou play with him as with a bird?

41:5 Wilt thou bind him for thy maidens?

41:6 Shall the companions make a banquet of him?

41:6 Shall they part him among the merchants?

41:7 Canst thou fill his skin with barbed irons?

41:7 Or his head with fish spears?

41:9 Shall not one be cast down even at the sight of him?

41:10 Who then is able to stand before me?

41:11 Who hath prevented me, that I should repay him?

41:13 Who can discover the face of his garment?

41:13 Who can come to him with his double bridle?

41:14 Who can open the doors of his face?

42:3 Who is he that hideth counsel without knowledge?

The Book of
Psalms

2:1 Why do the heathen rage, and the people imagine a vain thing?

4:2 How long will ye turn my glory into shame?

4:2 How long will ye love vanity, and seek after leasing?

4:6 Who will shew us any good?

6:3 My soul is also sore vexed: but thou, O LORD, how long?

6:5 In the grave who shall give thee thanks?

8:4 What is man, that thou art mindful of him?

8:4 And the son of man, that thou visitest him?

10:1 Why standest thou afar off, O LORD?

10:1 Why hidest thou thyself in times of trouble?

10:13 Wherefore doth the wicked contemn God?

11:1 In the LORD put I my trust: how say ye to my soul, Flee as a bird to your mountain?

11:3 If the foundations be destroyed, what can the righteous do?

12:4 Who have said, With our tongue will we prevail; our lips are our own: who is lord over us?

13:1 How long wilt thou forget me, O LORD?

13:1 For ever?

13:1 How long wilt thou hide thy face from me?

13:2 How long shall I take counsel in my soul, having sorrow in my heart daily?

13:2 How long shall mine enemy be exalted over me?

14:4 Have all the workers of iniquity no knowledge?

15:1 LORD, who shall abide in thy tabernacle?

15:1 Who shall dwell in thy holy hill?

18:31 For who is God save the LORD?

18:31 Who is a rock save our God?

19:12 Who can understand his errors?

22:1 My God, my God, why hast thou forsaken me?

22:1 Why art thou so far from helping me, and from the words of my roaring?

24:3 Who shall ascend into the hill of the LORD?

24:3 Who shall stand in his holy place?

24:8 Who is this King of glory?

24:9 Who is this King of glory?

25:12 What man is he that feareth the LORD?

27:1 The LORD is my light and my salvation; whom shall I fear?

27:1 The LORD is the strength of my life; of whom shall I be afraid?

30:9 What profit is there in my blood, when I go down to the pit?

30:9 Shall the dust praise thee?

30:9 Shall it declare thy truth?

34:12 What man is he that desireth life, and loveth many days, that he may see good?

35:10 All my bones shall say, LORD, who is like unto thee, which deliverest the poor from him that is too strong for him, yea, the poor and the needy from him that spoileth him?

35:17 Lord, how long wilt thou look on?

39:7 And now, Lord, what wait I for?

41:5 Mine enemies speak evil of me, When shall he die, and his name perish?

42:2 My soul thirsteth for God, for the living God: when shall I come and appear before God?

42:3 My tears have been my meat day and night, while they continually say unto me, Where is thy God?

42:5 Why art thou cast down, O my soul?

42:5 Why art thou disquieted in me?

42:9 I will say unto God my rock, Why hast thou forgotten me?

42:9 Why go I mourning because of the oppression of the enemy?

42:10 As with a sword in my bones, mine enemies reproach me; while they say daily unto me, Where is thy God?

42:11 Why art thou cast down, O my soul?

42:11 And why art thou disquieted within me?

43:2 For thou art the God of my strength: why dost thou cast me off?

43:2 Why go I mourning because of the oppression of the enemy?

43:5 Why art thou cast down, O my soul?

43:5 And why art thou disquieted within me?

44:21 Shall not God search this out?

44:23 Awake, why sleepest thou, O Lord?

44:24 Wherefore hidest thou thy face, and forgettest our affliction and our oppression?

49:5 Wherefore should I fear in the days of evil, when the iniquity of my heels shall compass me about?

50:13 Will I eat the flesh of bulls, or drink the blood of goats?

50:16 What hast thou to do to declare my statutes, or that thou shouldest take my covenant in thy mouth?

52:1 Why boastest thou thyself in mischief, O mighty man?

53:4 Have the workers of iniquity no knowledge?

54:1 Doth not David hide himself with us?

56:7 Shall they escape by iniquity?

56:8 Put thou my tears into thy bottle: are they not in thy book?

56:13 Wilt not thou deliver my feet from falling, that I may walk before God in the light of the living?

58:1 Do ye indeed speak righteousness, O congregation?

58:1 do ye judge uprightly, O ye sons of men?

59:7 Who, say they, doth hear?

60:9 Who will bring me into the strong city?

60:9 Who will lead me into Edom?

60:10 Wilt not thou, O God, which hadst cast us off?

60:10 Which didst not go out with our armies?

62:3 How long will ye imagine mischief against a man?

64:5 Who shall see them?

68:16 Why leap ye, ye high hills?

73:11 How doth God know?

73:11 Is there knowledge in the most High?

73:25 Whom have I in heaven but thee?

74:1 Why hast thou cast us off for ever?

74:1 Why doth thine anger smoke against the sheep of thy pasture?

74:10 How long shall the adversary reproach?

74:10 Shall the enemy blaspheme thy name for ever?

74:11 Why withdrawest thou thy hand, even thy right hand?

76:7 Who may stand in thy sight when once thou art angry?

77:7 Will the Lord cast off for ever?

77:7 Will he be favourable no more?

77:8 Is his mercy clean gone for ever?

77:8 Doth his promise fail for evermore?

77:9 Hath God forgotten to be gracious?

77:9 Hath he in anger shut up his tender mercies?

77:13 Who is so great a God as our God?

78:19 Yea, they spake against God; they said, Can God furnish a table in the wilderness?

78:20 Can he give bread also?

78:20 Can he provide flesh for his people?

79:5 How long, LORD?

79:5 Wilt thou be angry for ever?

79:5 Shall thy jealousy burn like fire?

79:10 Where is their God?

80:4 How long wilt thou be angry against the prayer of thy people?

80:12 Why hast thou then broken down her hedges, so that all they which pass by the way do pluck her?

82:2 How long will ye judge unjustly, and accept the persons of the wicked?

85:5 Wilt thou be angry with us for ever?

85:5 Wilt thou draw out thine anger to all generations?

85:6 Wilt thou not revive us again: that thy people may rejoice in thee?

88:10 Wilt thou shew wonders to the dead?

88:10 Shall the dead arise and praise thee?

88:11 Shall thy lovingkindness be declared in the grave?

88:11 Or thy faithfulness in destruction?

88:12 Shall thy wonders be known in the dark?

88:12 And thy righteousness in the land of forgetfulness?

88:14 Why castest thou off my soul?

88:14 Why hidest thou thy face from me?

89:6 Who in the heaven can be compared unto the LORD?

89:6 Who among the sons of the mighty can be likened unto the LORD?

89:8 Who is a strong LORD like unto thee?

89:8 Or to thy faithfulness round about thee?

89:46 How long, LORD?

89:46 Wilt thou hide thyself for ever?

89:46 Shall thy wrath burn like fire?

89:47 Wherefore hast thou made all men in vain?

89:48 What man is he that liveth, and shall not see death?

89:48 Shall he deliver his soul from the hand of the grave?

89:49 Where are thy former lovingkindnesses, which thou swarest unto David in thy truth?

90:11 Who knoweth the power of thine anger?

90:13 How long?

94:3 How long shall the wicked, how long shall the wicked triumph?

94:4 How long shall they utter and speak hard things?

94:4 And all the workers of iniquity boast themselves?

94:8 When will ye be wise?

94:9 He that planted the ear, shall he not hear?

94:9 He that formed the eye, shall he not see?

94:10 He that chastiseth the heathen, shall not he correct?

94:10 He that teacheth man knowledge, shall not he know?

94:16 Who will rise up for me against the evildoers?

94:16 Who will stand up for me against the workers of iniquity?

94:20 Shall the throne of iniquity have fellowship with thee, which frameth mischief by a law?

101:2 When wilt thou come unto me?

106:2 Who can utter the mighty acts of the LORD?

106:2 Who can shew forth all his praise?

108:10 Who will bring me into the strong city?

108:10 Who will lead me into Edom?

108:11 Wilt not thou, O God, who hast cast us off?

108:11 Wilt not thou, O God, go forth with our hosts?

114:5 What ailed thee, O thou sea, that thou fleddest?

114:5 Thou Jordan, that thou wast driven back?

114:6 Ye mountains, that ye skipped like rams; and ye little hills, like lambs?

115:2 Wherefore should the heathen say, Where is now their God?

116:12 What shall I render unto the LORD for all his benefits toward me?

118:6 The LORD is on my side; I will not fear: what can man do unto me?

119:82 When wilt thou comfort me?

119:84 How many are the days of thy servant?

119:84 When wilt thou execute judgment on them that persecute me?

120:3 What shall be given unto thee?

120:3 What shall be done unto thee, thou false tongue?

130:3 If thou, LORD, shouldest mark iniquities, O Lord, who shall stand?

137:4 How shall we sing the LORD'S song in a strange land?

139:7 Whither shall I go from thy spirit?

139:7 Whither shall I flee from thy presence?

139:21 Do not I hate them, O LORD, that hate thee?

139:21 Am not I grieved with those that rise up against thee?

147:17 Who can stand before his cold?

The
Proverbs

1:22 How long, ye simple ones, will ye love simplicity?

1:22 And the scorners delight in their scorning, and fools hate knowledge?

5:20 And why wilt thou, my son, be ravished with a strange woman, and embrace the bosom of a stranger?

6:9 How long wilt thou sleep, O sluggard?

6:9 When wilt thou arise out of thy sleep?

6:27 Can a man take fire in his bosom, and his clothes not be burned?

6:28 Can one go upon hot coals, and his feet not be burned?

8:1 Doth not wisdom cry?

8:1 And understanding put forth her voice?

15:11 Hell and destruction are before the LORD: how much more then the hearts of the children of men?

17:16 Wherefore is there a price in the hand of a fool to get wisdom, seeing he hath no heart to it?

18:14 The spirit of a man will sustain his infirmity; but a wounded spirit who can bear?

19:7 All the brethren of the poor do hate him: how much more do his friends go far from him?

20:6 Most men will proclaim every one his own goodness: but a faithful man who can find?

20:9 Who can say, I have made my heart clean, I am pure from my sin?

20:24 Man's goings are of the LORD; how can a man then understand his own way?

21:27 The sacrifice of the wicked is abomination: how much more, when he bringeth it with a wicked mind?

22:27 If thou hast nothing to pay, why should he take away thy bed from under thee?

22:20, 21 Have not I written to thee excellent things in counsels and knowledge, That I might make thee know the certainty of the words of truth; that thou mightest answer the words of truth to them that send unto thee?

22:29 Seest thou a man diligent in his business? he shall stand before kings; he shall not stand before mean men.

23:5 Wilt thou set thine eyes upon that which is not? for riches certainly make themselves wings; they fly away as an eagle toward heaven.

23:29 Who hath woe?

23:29 Who hath sorrow?

23:29 Who hath contentions?

23:29 Who hath babbling?

23:29 Who hath wounds without cause?

23:29 Who hath redness of eyes?

23:35 They have stricken me, shalt thou say, and I was not sick; they have beaten me, and I felt it not: when shall I awake? I will seek it yet again.

24:12 If thou sayest, Behold, we knew it not; doth not he that pondereth the heart consider it?

24:12 And he that keepeth thy soul, doth not he know it?

24:12 And shall not he render to everyman according to his works?

24:22 For their calamity shall rise suddenly; and who knoweth the ruin of them both?

25:16 Hast thou found honey? eat so much as is sufficient for thee, lest thou be filled therewith, and vomit it.

26:18, 19 As a mad man who casteth firebrands, arrows, and death, So is the man that deceiveth his neighbour, and saith, Am not I in sport?

27:4 Wrath is cruel, and anger is outrageous; but who is able to stand before envy?

27:24 For riches are not for ever: and doth the crown endure to every generation?

29:20 Seest thou a man that is hasty in his words? there is more hope of a fool than of him.

30:4 Who hath ascended up into heaven, or descended?

30:4 Who hath gathered the wind in his fists?

30:4 Who hath bound the waters in a garment?

30:4 Who hath established all the ends of the earth?

30:4 What is his name, and what is his son's name, if thou canst tell?

30:7, 9 Two things have I required of thee; deny me them not before I die: Remove far from me vanity and lies: give me neither poverty nor riches; feed me with food convenient for me: Lest I be full, and deny thee, and say, Who is the LORD? or lest I be poor, and steal, and take the name of my God in vain.

31:2 What, my son?

31:2 What, the son of my womb?

31:2 What, the son of my vows?

31:10 Who can find a virtuous woman? for her price is far above rubies.

Ecclesiastes or the Preacher

1:3 What profit hath a man of all his labour which he taketh under the sun?

2:2 What doeth it?

2:12 What can the man do that cometh after the king?

2:15 Then said I in my heart, As it happeneth to the fool, so it happeneth even to me; and why was I then more wise? Then I said in my heart, that this also is vanity.

2:16 How dieth the wise man?

2:19 Who knoweth whether he shall be a wise man or a fool?

2:22 What hath man of all his labour, and of the vexation of his heart, wherein he hath laboured under the sun?

2:25 For who can eat, or who else can hasten hereunto, more than I?

3:9 What profit hath he that worketh in that wherein he laboureth?

3:21 Who knoweth the spirit of man that goeth upward, and the spirit of the beast that goeth downward to the earth?

3:22 Wherefore I perceive that there is nothing better, than that a man should rejoice in his own works; for that is his portion: for who shall bring him to see what shall be after him?

4:8 For whom do I labour, and bereave my soul of good?

4:11 How can one be warm alone?

5:6 Wherefore should God be angry at thy voice, and destroy the work of thine hands?

5:11 When goods increase, they are increased that eat them: and what good is there to the owners thereof, saving the beholding of them with their eyes?

5:16 What profit hath he that hath laboured for the wind?

6:6 Do not all go to one place?

6:8 For what hath the wise more than the fool?

6:8 What hath the poor, that knoweth to walk before the living?

6:11 What is man the better?

6:12 For who knoweth what is good for man in this life, all the days of his vain life which he spendeth as a shadow?

6:12 for who can tell a man what shall be after him under the sun?

7:10 What is the cause that the former days were better than these?

7:13 Who can make that straight, which he hath made crooked?

7:16 Why shouldest thou destroy thyself?

7:17 Why shouldest thou die before thy time?

7:24 Who can find it out?

8:1 Who is as the wise man?

8:1 Who knoweth the interpretation of a thing?

8:4 Who may say unto him, What doest thou?

8:7 Who can tell him when it shall be?

8:19 And when they shall say unto you, Seek unto them that have familiar spirits, and unto wizards that peep, and that mutter: should not a people seek unto their God?

8:19 for the living to the dead?

10:14 What shall be after him, who can tell him?

The
Song of Solomon

3:3 Saw ye him whom my soul loveth?

3:6 Who is this that cometh out of the wilderness like pillars of smoke, perfumed with myrrh and frankincense, with all powders of the merchant?

5:3 How shall I put it on?

5:3 How shall I defile them?

5:9 What is thy beloved more than another beloved, O thou fairest among women?

5:9 What is thy beloved more than another beloved, that thou dost so charge us?

6:1 Whither is thy beloved gone, O thou fairest among women?

6:1 Whither is thy beloved turned aside?

6:10 Who is she that looketh forth as the morning, fair as the moon, clear as the sun, and terrible as an army with banners?

6:13 What will ye see in the Shulamite?

8:5 Who is this that cometh up from the wilderness, leaning upon her beloved?

8:8 What shall we do for our sister in the day when she shall be spoken for?

Saw ye him whom my soul loveth?
Song of Solomon 3:3

MAJOR PROPHETS

Shall the work say of him that made it, He made me not?
Isaiah 29:16

The Book of the Prophet
Isaiah

1:5 Why should ye be stricken any more?

1:11 What purpose is the multitude of your sacrifices unto me?

1:12 When ye come to appear before me, who hath required this at your hand, to tread my courts?

2:22 Wherein is he to be accounted of?

5:4 What could have been done more to my vineyard, that I have not done in it?

5:4 When I looked that it should bring forth grapes, brought it forth wild grapes?

6:8 Whom shall I send, and who will go for us?

7:13 Will ye weary my God also?

10:3 What will ye do in the day of visitation, and in the desolation which shall come from far?

10:3 To whom will ye flee for help?

10:3 Where will ye leave your glory?

10:8 Are not my princes altogether kings?

10:9 Is not Calno as Carchemish?

10:9 Is not Hamath as Arpad?

10:9 Is not Samaria as Damascus?

10:11 Shall I not, as I have done unto Samaria and her idols, so do to Jerusalem and her idols?

10:15 Shall the axe boast itself against him that heweth therewith?

10:15 Shall the saw magnify itself against him that shaketh it?

14:10 Art thou also become weak as we?

14:10 Art thou become like unto us?

14:17 Is this the man that made the earth to tremble, that did shake kingdoms; That made the world as a wilderness, and destroyed the cities thereof; that opened not the house of his prisoners?

14:27 Who shall disannul it?

14:27 Who shall turn it back?

14:32 What shall one then answer the messengers of the nation?

19:11 How say ye unto Pharaoh, I am the son of the wise, the son of ancient kings?

19:12 Where are they?

19:12 Where are thy wise men?

20:6 How shall we escape?

21:11 Watchman, what of the night?

21:11 Watchman, what of the night?

22:1 What aileth thee now, that thou art wholly gone up to the housetops?

22:16 What hast thou here?

22:16 Whom hast thou here, that thou hast hewed thee out a sepulchre here, as he that heweth him out a sepulchre on high, and that graveth an habitation for himself in a rock?

23:7 Is this your joyous city, whose antiquity is of ancient days?

23:8 Who hath taken this counsel against Tyre, the crowning city, whose merchants are princes, whose traffickers are the honourable of the earth?

27:4 Who would set the briers and thorns against me in battle?

27:7 Hath he smitten him, as he smote those that smote him?

27:7 Is he slain according to the slaughter of them that are slain by him?

28:9 Whom shall he teach knowledge?

28:9 Whom shall he make to understand doctrine?

28:24 Doth the plowman plow all day to sow?

28:25 Doth he open and break the clods of his ground?

28:25 When he hath made plain the face thereof, doth he not cast abroad the fitches, and scatter the cummin, and cast in the principal wheat and the appointed barley and the rie in their place?

29:15 Who seeth us?

29:15 Who knoweth us?

29:16 Shall the work say of him that made it, He made me not?

29:16 Shall the thing framed say of him that framed it, He had no understanding?

29:17 Is it not yet a very little while, and Lebanon shall be turned into a fruitful field, and the fruitful field shall be esteemed as a forest?

33:14 Who among us shall dwell with the devouring fire?

33:14 Who among us shall dwell with everlasting burnings?

33:18 Where is the scribe?

33:18 Where is the receiver?

33:18 Where is he that counted the towers?

36:4 What confidence is this wherein thou trustest?

36:5 On whom dost thou trust, that thou rebellest against me?

36:7 We trust in the LORD our God: is it not he, whose high places and whose altars Hezekiah hath taken away, and said to Judah and to Jerusalem, Ye shall worship before this altar?

36:9 How then wilt thou turn away the face of one captain of the least of my master's servants, and put thy trust on Egypt for chariots and for horsemen?

36:10 Am I now come up without the LORD against this land to destroy it?

36:12 Hath my master sent me to thy master and to thee to speak these words?

36:12 Hath he not sent me to the men that sit upon the wall, that they may eat their own dung, and drink their own piss with you?

36:18 Hath any of the gods of the nations delivered his land out of the hand of the king of Assyria?

36:19 Where are the gods of Sepharvaim?

36:19 Have they delivered Samaria out of my hand?

36:20 Who are they among all the gods of these lands, that have delivered their land out of my hand, that the LORD should deliver Jerusalem out of my hand?

37:11 Shalt thou be delivered?

37:12 Have the gods of the nations delivered them which my fathers have destroyed, as Gozan, and Haran, and Rezeph, and the children of Eden which were in Telassar?

37:13 Where is the king of Hamath, and the king of Arphad, and the king of the city of Sepharvaim, Hena, and Ivah?

37:23 Whom hast thou reproached and blasphemed?

37:23 Against whom hast thou exalted thy voice, and lifted up thine eyes on high?

37:26 Hast thou not heard long ago, how I have done it; and of ancient times, that I have formed it?

38:15 What shall I say?

38:22 What is the sign that I shall go up to the house of the LORD?

39:3 What said these men?

39:3 From whence came they unto thee?

39:4 What have they seen in thine house?

39:19 Where are the gods of Hamath and Arphad?

40:6 What shall I cry?

40:12 Who hath measured the waters in the hollow of his hand, and meted out heaven with the span, and comprehended the dust of the earth in a measure weighed the mountains in scales, and the hills in a balance?

40:13 Who hath directed the Spirit of the LORD, or being his counsellor hath taught him?

40:14 With whom took he counsel, and who instructed him, and taught him in the path of judgment, and taught him knowledge, and shewed to him the way of understanding?

40:18 To whom then will ye liken God?

40:18 What likeness will ye compare unto him?

40:21 Have ye not known?

40:21 Have ye not heard?

40:21 Hath it not been told you from the beginning?

40:21 Have ye not understood from the foundations of the earth?

40:25 To whom then will ye liken me, or shall I be equal? saith the Holy One.

40:27 Why sayest thou, O Jacob, and speakest, O Israel, My way is hid from the LORD, and my judgment is passed over from my God?

40:28 Hast thou not known?

40:28 Hast thou not heard, that the everlasting God, the LORD, the Creator of the ends of the earth, fainteth not, neither is weary?

41:2 Who raised up the righteous man from the east, called him to his foot, gave the nations before him, and made him rule over kings?

41:4 Who hath wrought and done it, calling the generations from the beginning?

41:26 Who hath declared from the beginning, that we may know?

41:26 And before time, that we may say, He is righteous?

42:19 Who is blind, but my servant?

42:19 Or deaf, as my messenger that I sent?

42:19 Who is blind as he that is perfect, and blind as the LORD'S servant?

42:23 Who among you will give ear to this?

42:23 Who will hearken and hear for the time to come?

42:24 Who gave Jacob for a spoil, and Israel to the robbers?

42:24 Did not the LORD, he against whom we have sinned?

43:9 Who among them can declare this, and shew us former things?

43:13 Who shall let it?

43:19 Shall ye not know it?

44:7 Who, as I, shall call, and shall declare it, and set it in order for me, since I appointed the ancient people?

44:8 Have not I told thee from that time, and have declared it?

44:8 Is there a God beside me?

44:10 Who hath formed a god, or molten a graven image that is profitable for nothing?

44:19 Shall I make the residue thereof an abomination?

44:19 Shall I fall down to the stock of a tree?

44:20 Is there not a lie in my right hand?

45:9 Shall the clay say to him that fashioneth it, What makest thou?

45:9 or thy work, He hath no hands?

45:10 What begettest thou?

45:10 What hast thou brought forth?

45:21 Who hath declared this from ancient time?

45:21 Who hath told it from that time?

45:21 Have not I the LORD?

46:5 To whom will ye liken me, and make me equal, and compare me, that we may be like?

48:6 Will not ye declare it?

48:11 How should my name be polluted?

48:14 Which among them hath declared these things?

49:15 Can a woman forget her sucking child, that she should not have compassion on the son of her womb?

49:21 Who hath begotten me these, seeing I have lost my children, and am desolate, a captive, and removing to and fro?

49:21 Who hath brought up these?

49:21 Where had they been?

49:24 Shall the prey be taken from the mighty, or the lawful captive delivered?

50:1 Where is the bill of your mother's divorcement, whom I have put away?

50:1 Which of my creditors is it to whom I have sold you?

50:2 Wherefore, when I came, was there no man?

50:2 When I called, was there none to answer?

50:2 Is my hand shortened at all, that it cannot redeem?

50:2 Have I no power to deliver?

50:8 Who will contend with me?

50:8 Who is mine adversary?

50:9 Who is he that shall condemn me?

50:10 Who is among you that feareth the LORD, that obeyeth the voice of his servant, that walketh in darkness, and hath no light?

51:9 Art thou not it that hath cut Rahab, and wounded the dragon?

51:10 Art thou not it which hath dried the sea, the waters of the great deep; that hath made the depths of the sea a way for the ransomed to pass over?

51:13 Where is the fury of the oppressor?

51:19 Who shall be sorry for thee?

51:19 By whom shall I comfort thee?

51:12, 13 Who art thou, that thou shouldest be afraid of a man that shall die, and of the son of man which shall be made as grass; And forgettest the LORD thy maker, that hath stretched forth the heavens, and laid the foundations of the earth; and hast feared continually every day because of the fury of the oppressor, as if he were ready to destroy?

52:5 What have I here, saith the LORD, that my people is taken away for nought?

53:1 Who hath believed our report?

53:1 And to whom is the arm of the LORD revealed?

53:8 Who shall declare his generation?

55:2 Wherefore do ye spend money for that which is not bread?

55:2 And your labour for that which satisfieth not?

57:4 Against whom do ye sport yourselves?

57:4 Against whom make ye a wide mouth, and draw out the tongue?

57:4, 5 Are ye not children of transgression, a seed of falsehood, Enflaming yourselves with idols under every green tree, slaying the children in the valleys under the clifts of the rocks?

57:6 Should I receive comfort in these?

57:11 Whom hast thou been afraid or feared, that thou hast lied, and hast not remembered me, nor laid it to thy heart?

57:11 Have not I held my peace even of old, and thou fearest me not?

58:3 Wherefore have we fasted, say they, and thou seest not?

58:3 Wherefore have we afflicted our soul, and thou takest no knowledge?

58:5 Is it such a fast that I have chosen?

58:5 A day for a man to afflict his soul?

58:5 Is it to bow down his head as a bulrush, and to spread sackcloth and ashes under him?

58:5 Wilt thou call this a fast, and an acceptable day to the LORD?

58:6 Is not this the fast that I have chosen?

58:6 To loose the bands of wickedness, to undo the heavy burdens, and to let the oppressed go free, and that ye break every yoke?

58:7 Is it not to deal thy bread to the hungry, and that thou bring the poor that are cast out to thy house?

58:7 When thou seest the naked, that thou cover him; and that thou hide not thyself from thine own flesh?

60:8 Who are these that fly as a cloud, and as the doves to their windows?

63:1 Who is this that cometh from Edom, with dyed garments from Bozrah?

63:1 This that is glorious in his apparel, travelling in the greatness of his strength?

63:2 Wherefore art thou red in thine apparel, and thy garments like him that treadeth in the winefat?

63:11 Where is he that brought them up out of the sea with the shepherd of his flock?

63:11 Where is he that put his holy Spirit within him?

63:12 That led them by the right hand of Moses with his glorious arm, dividing the water before them, to make himself an everlasting name?

63:13 That led them through the deep, as an horse in the wilderness, that they should not stumble?

63:15 Where is thy zeal and thy strength, the sounding of thy bowels and of thy mercies toward me?

63:15 Are they restrained?

63:17 Why hast thou made us to err from thy ways, and hardened our heart from thy fear?

64:12 Wilt thou refrain thyself for these things, O LORD?

64:12 Wilt thou hold thy peace, and afflict us very sore?

66:1 Where is the house that ye build unto me?

66:1 Where is the place of my rest?

66:8 Who hath heard such a thing?

66:8 Who hath seen such things?

66:8 Shall the earth be made to bring forth in one day?

66:8 Shall a nation be born at once?

66:9 Shall I bring to the birth, and not cause to bring forth?

66:9 Shall I cause to bring forth, and shut the womb?

The Book of the Prophet
Jeremiah

1:11 What seest thou?

1:13 What seest thou?

2:5 What iniquity have your fathers found in me, that they are gone far from me, and have walked after vanity, and are become vain?

2:6 Where is the LORD that brought us up out of the land of Egypt, that led us through the wilderness, through a land of deserts and of pits, through a land of drought, and of the shadow of death, through a land that no man passed through, and where no man dwelt?

2:8 Where is the LORD?

2:11 Hath a nation changed their gods, which are yet no gods?

2:14 Is Israel a servant?

2:14 Is he a homeborn slave?

2:14 Why is he spoiled?

2:17 Hast thou not procured this unto thyself, in that thou hast forsaken the LORD thy God, when he led thee by the way?

2:18 what hast thou to do in the way of Egypt, to drink the waters of Sihor?

2:18 What hast thou to do in the way of Assyria, to drink the waters of the river?

2:21 How then art thou turned into the degenerate plant of a strange vine unto me?

2:23 How canst thou say, I am not polluted, I have not gone after Baalim?

2:24 Who can turn her away?

2:28 Where are thy gods that thou hast made thee?

2:29 Wherefore will ye plead with me?

2:31 Have I been a wilderness unto Israel?

2:31 A land of darkness?

2:31 Wherefore say my people, We are lords; we will come no more unto thee?

2:32 Can a maid forget her ornaments, or a bride her attire?

2:33 Why trimmest thou thy way to seek love?

2:36 Why gaddest thou about so much to change thy way?

3:1 If a man put away his wife, and she go from him, and become another man's, shall he return unto her again?

3:1 Shall not that land be greatly polluted?

3:4 Wilt thou not from this time cry unto me, My father, thou art the guide of my youth?

3:5 Will he reserve his anger for ever?

3:5 Will he keep it to the end?

3:6 Hast thou seen that which backsliding Israel hath done?

3:19 How shall I put thee among the children, and give thee a pleasant land, a goodly heritage of the hosts of nations?

4:14 How long shall thy vain thoughts lodge within thee?

4:21 How long shall I see the standard, and hear the sound of the trumpet?

4:30 When thou art spoiled, what wilt thou do?

5:3 O LORD, are not thine eyes upon the truth?

5:7 How shall I pardon thee for this?

5:9 Shall I not visit for these things?

5:9 Shall not my soul be avenged on such a nation as this?

5:19 Wherefore doeth the LORD our God all these things unto us?

5:22 Fear ye not me?

5:22 Will ye not tremble at my presence, which have placed the sand for the bound of the sea by a perpetual decree, that it cannot pass it: and though the waves thereof toss themselves, yet can they not prevail; though they roar, yet can they not pass over it?

5:29 Shall I not visit for these things?

5:29 Shall not my soul be avenged on such a nation as this?

5:31 What will ye do in the end thereof?

6:10 To whom shall I speak, and give warning, that they may hear?

6:15 Were they ashamed when they had committed abomination?

6:20 To what purpose cometh there to me incense from Sheba, and the sweet cane from a far country?

7:9,10 Will ye steal, murder, and commit adultery, and swear falsely, and burn incense unto Baal, and walk after other gods whom ye know not; And come and stand before me in this house, which is called by my name, and say, We are delivered to do all these abominations?

7:11 Is this house, which is called by my name, become a den of robbers in your eyes?

7:17 Seest thou not what they do in the cities of Judah and in the streets of Jerusalem?

7:19 Do they provoke me to anger?

7:19 Do they not provoke themselves to the confusion of their own faces?

8:4 Shall they fall, and not arise?

8:4 Shall he turn away, and not return?

8:5 Why then is this people of Jerusalem slidden back by a perpetual backsliding?

8:6 What have I done?

8:8 How do ye say, We are wise, and the law of the LORD is with us?

8:9 What wisdom is in them?

8:12 Were they ashamed when they had committed abomination?

8:14 Why do we sit still?

8:19 Is not the LORD in Zion?

8:19 Is not her king in her?

8:19 Why have they provoked me to anger with their graven images, and with strange vanities?

8:22 Is there no balm in Gilead; is there no physician there?

8:22 Why then is not the health of the daughter of my people recovered?

9:7 How shall I do for the daughter of my people?

9:9 Shall I not visit them for these things?

9:9 Shall not my soul be avenged on such a nation as this?

9:12 Who is the wise man, that may understand this?

9:12 Who is he to whom the mouth of the LORD hath spoken, that he may declare it, for what the land perisheth and is burned up like a wilderness, that none passeth through?

10:7 Who would not fear thee, O King of nations?

11:15 What hath my beloved to do in mine house, seeing she hath wrought lewdness with many, and the holy flesh is passed from thee?

12:1 Wherefore doth the way of the wicked prosper?

12:1 Wherefore are all they happy that deal very treacherously?

12:4 How long shall the land mourn, and the herbs of every field wither, for the wickedness of them that dwell therein?

12:5 If thou hast run with the footmen, and they have wearied thee, then how canst thou contend with horses?

12:5 If in the land of peace, wherein thou trustedst, they wearied thee, then how wilt thou do in the swelling of Jordan?

13:12 Do we not certainly know that every bottle shall be filled with wine?

13:20 Where is the flock that was given thee, thy beautiful flock?

13:21 What wilt thou say when he shall punish thee?

13:21 Shall not sorrows take thee, as a woman in travail?

13:22 Wherefore come these things upon me?

13:23 Can the Ethiopian change his skin, or the leopard his spots?

13:27 Wilt thou not be made clean?

13:27 When shall it once be?

14:8 Why shouldest thou be as a stranger in the land, and as a wayfaring man that turneth aside to tarry for a night?

14:9 Why shouldest thou be as a man astonied, as a mighty man that cannot save?

14:19 Hast thou utterly rejected Judah?

14:19 Hath thy soul lothed Zion?

14:19 Why hast thou smitten us, and there is no healing for us?

14:22 Are there any among the vanities of the Gentiles that can cause rain?

14:22 Can the heavens give showers?

14:22 Art not thou he, O LORD our God?

15:2 Whither shall we go forth?

15:5 For who shall have pity upon thee, O Jerusalem?

15:5 Who shall bemoan thee?

15:5 Who shall go aside to ask how thou doest?

15:12 Shall iron break the northern iron and the steel?

15:18 Why is my pain perpetual, and my wound incurable, which refuseth to be healed?

15:18 Wilt thou be altogether unto me as a liar, and as waters that fail?

16:10 Wherefore hath the LORD pronounced all this great evil against us?

16:10 What is our iniquity?

16:10 What is our sin that we have committed against the LORD our God?

16:20 Shall a man make gods unto himself, and they are no gods?

17:9 The heart is deceitful above all things, and desperately wicked: who can know it?

17:15 Where is the word of the LORD?

18:6 Cannot I do with you as this potter?

18:14 Will a man leave the snow of Lebanon which cometh from the rock of the field?

18:14 Shall the cold flowing waters that come from another place be forsaken?

18:20 Shall evil be recompensed for good?

20:18 Wherefore came I forth out of the womb to see labour and sorrow, that my days should be consumed with shame?

21:13 Who shall come down against us?

21:13 Who shall enter into our habitations?

22:8 Wherefore hath the LORD done thus unto this great city?

22:15 Shalt thou reign, because thou closest thyself in cedar?

22:15 Did not thy father eat and drink, and do judgment and justice, and then it was well with him?

22:16 He judged the cause of the poor and needy; then it was well with him: was not this to know me? saith the LORD.

22:28 Is this man Coniah a despised broken idol?

22:28 Is he a vessel wherein is no pleasure?

22:28 Wherefore are they cast out, he and his seed, and are cast into a land which they know not?

23:18 Who hath stood in the counsel of the LORD, and hath perceived and heard his word?

23:18 Who hath marked his word, and heard it?

23:23 Am I a God at hand, saith the LORD, and not a God afar off?

23:24 Can any hide himself in secret places that I shall not see him?

23:24 Do not I fill heaven and earth?

23:26 How long shall this be in the heart of the prophets that prophesy lies?

23:28 What is the chaff to the wheat?

23:29 Is not my word like as a fire?

23:29 And like a hammer that breaketh the rock in pieces?

23:33 What is the burden of the LORD?

23:33 What burden?

23:35 What hath the LORD answered?

23:35 What hath the LORD spoken?

23:37 What hath the LORD answered thee?

23:37 What hath the LORD spoken?

24:3 What seest thou, Jeremiah?

25:29 Should ye be utterly unpunished?

26:9 Why hast thou prophesied in the name of the LORD, saying, This house shall be like Shiloh, and this city shall be desolate without an inhabitant?

26:19 Did Hezekiah king of Judah and all Judah put him at all to death?

26:19 Did he not fear the LORD, and besought the LORD, and the LORD repented him of the evil which he had pronounced against them?

27:13 Why will ye die, thou and thy people, by the sword, by the famine, and by the pestilence, as the LORD hath spoken against the nation that will not serve the king of Babylon?

27:17 Wherefore should this city be laid waste?

29:27 Why hast thou not reproved Jeremiah of Anathoth, which maketh himself a prophet to you?

30:6 Ask ye now, and see whether a man doth travail with child?

30:6 Wherefore do I see every man with his hands on his loins, as a woman in travail, and all faces are turned into paleness?

30:15 Why criest thou for thine affliction?

30:21 For who is this that engaged his heart to approach unto me? saith the LORD.

31:20 Is Ephraim my dear son?

31:20 Is he a pleasant child?

31:22 How long wilt thou go about, O thou backsliding daughter?

32:27 Is there any thing too hard for me?

33:24 Considerest thou not what this people have spoken, saying, The two families which the LORD hath chosen, he hath even cast them off?

35:13 Will ye not receive instruction to hearken to my words?

36:17 How didst thou write all these words at his mouth?

36:29 Why hast thou written therein, saying, The king of Babylon shall certainly come and destroy this land, and shall cause to cease from thence man and beast?

37:17 Is there any word from the LORD?

37:18 What have I offended against thee, or against thy servants, or against this people, that ye have put me in prison?

37:19 Where are now your prophets which prophesied unto you, saying, The king of Babylon shall not come against you, nor against this land?

38:15 If I declare it unto thee, wilt thou not surely put me to death?

38:15 If I give thee counsel, wilt thou not hearken unto me?

40:14 Dost thou certainly know that Baalis the king of the Ammonites hath sent Ishmael the son of Nethaniah to slay thee?

40:15 Wherefore should he slay thee, that all the Jews which are gathered unto thee should be scattered, and the remnant in Judah perish?

44:9 Have ye forgotten the wickedness of your fathers, and the wickedness of the kings of Judah, and the wickedness of their wives, and your own wickedness, and the wickedness of your wives, which they have committed in the land of Judah, and in the streets of Jerusalem?

44:19 When we burned incense to the queen of heaven, and poured out drink offerings unto her, did we make her cakes to worship her, and pour out drink offerings unto her, without our men?

44:21 Did not the LORD remember them, and came it not into his mind?

44:7, 8 Wherefore commit ye this great evil against your souls, to cut off from you man and woman, child and suckling, out of Judah, to leave you none to remain; In that ye provoke me unto wrath with the works of your hands, burning incense unto other gods in the land of Egypt, whither ye be gone to dwell, that ye might cut yourselves off, and that ye might be a curse and a reproach among all the nations of the earth?

45:5 Seekest thou great things for thyself?

46:5 Wherefore have I seen them dismayed and turned away back?

46:7 Who is this that cometh up as a flood, whose waters are moved as the rivers?

46:15 Why are thy valiant men swept away?

47:5 How long wilt thou cut thyself?

47:6 How long will it be ere thou be quiet?

47:7 How can it be quiet, seeing the LORD hath given it a charge against Ashkelon, and against the sea shore?

48:14 How say ye, We are mighty and strong men for the war?

48:19 What is done?

48:27 For was not Israel a derision unto thee?

48:27 Was he found among thieves?

49:1 Hath Israel no sons?

49:1 Hath he no heir?

49:1 Why then doth their king inherit Gad, and his people dwell in his cities?

49:4 Wherefore gloriest thou in the valleys, thy flowing valley, O backsliding daughter?

49:4 Who shall come unto me?

49:7 Is wisdom no more in Teman?

49:7 Is counsel perished from the prudent?

49:7 Is their wisdom vanished?

49:9 If grape gatherers come to thee, would they not leave some gleaning grapes?

49:12 Art thou he that shall altogether go unpunished?

49:19 Who is a chosen man, that I may appoint over her?

49:19 Who is like me?

49:19 Who will appoint me the time?

49:19 Who is that shepherd that will stand before me?

50:44 Who is a chosen man, that I may appoint over her?

50:44 Who is like me?

50:44 Who will appoint me the time?

50:44 Who is that shepherd that will stand before me?

Lamentations of Jeremiah

1:12 Is it nothing to you, all ye that pass by?

2:12 Where is corn and wine?

2:13 What thing shall I take to witness for thee?

2:13 What thing shall I liken to thee, O daughter of Jerusalem?

2:13 What shall I equal to thee, that I may comfort thee, O virgin daughter of Zion?

2:13 Who can heal thee?

2:15 Is this the city that men call The perfection of beauty, The joy of the whole earth?

2:20 Shall the women eat their fruit, and children of a span long?

2:20 Shall the priest and the prophet be slain in the sanctuary of the Lord?

3:37 Who is he that saith, and it cometh to pass, when the Lord commandeth it not?

3:38 Out of the mouth of the most High proceedeth not evil and good?

3:39 Wherefore doth a living man complain, a man for the punishment of his sins?

5:20 Wherefore dost thou forget us for ever, and forsake us for so long time?

The Book of the Prophet
Ezekiel

8:6 Seest thou what they do?

8:6 Even the great abominations that the house of Israel committeth here, that I should go far off from my sanctuary?

8:12 Hast thou seen what the ancients of the house of Israel do in the dark, every man in the chambers of his imagery?

8:15 Hast thou seen this, O son of man? turn thee yet again, and thou shalt see greater abominations than these.

8:17 Hast thou seen this, O son of man?

8:17 Is it a light thing to the house of Judah that they commit the abominations which they commit here?

9:8 Wilt thou destroy all the residue of Israel in thy pouring out of thy fury upon Jerusalem?

11:13 Wilt thou make a full end of the remnant of Israel?

12:9 What doest thou?

12:22 What is that proverb that ye have in the land of Israel, saying, The days are prolonged, and every vision faileth?

13:7 Have ye not seen a vain vision, and have ye not spoken a lying divination, whereas ye say, The LORD saith it; albeit I have not spoken?

13:12 When the wall is fallen, shall it not be said unto you, Where is the daubing wherewith ye have daubed it?

13:18 Will ye hunt the souls of my people, and will ye save the souls alive that come unto you?

13:19 Will ye pollute me among my people for handfuls of barley and for pieces of bread, to slay the souls that should not die, and to save the souls alive that should not live, by your lying to my people that hear your lies?

14:3 Should I be enquired of at all by them?

14:21 How much more when I send my four sore judgments upon Jerusalem, the sword, and the famine, and the noisome beast, and the pestilence, to cut off from it man and beast?

15:2 What is the vine tree more than any tree, or than a branch which is among the trees of the forest?

15:3 Shall wood be taken thereof to do any work?

15:3 Will men take a pin of it to hang any vessel thereon?

15:4 Is it meet for any work?

15:5 When it was whole, it was meet for no work: how much less shall it be meet yet for any work, when the fire hath devoured it, and it is burned?

16:20, 21 Is this of thy whoredoms a small matter, That thou hast slain my children, and delivered them to cause them to pass through the fire for them?

17:9 Shall it prosper?

17:9 Shall he not pull up the roots thereof, and cut off the fruit thereof, that it wither?

17:10 Shall it prosper?

17:10 Shall it not utterly wither, when the east wind toucheth it?

17:12 Know ye not what these things mean?

17:15 Shall he prosper?

17:15 Shall he escape that doeth such things?

17:15 Shall he break the covenant, and be delivered?

18:2 What mean ye, that ye use this proverb concerning the land of Israel, saying, The fathers have eaten sour grapes, and the children's teeth are set on edge?

18:13 Shall he then live?

18:19 Why?

18:19 Doth not the son bear the iniquity of the father?

18:23 Have I any pleasure at all that the wicked should die?

18:23 And not that he should return from his ways, and live?

18:24 When the righteous turneth away from his righteousness, and committeth iniquity, and doeth according to all the abominations that the wicked man doeth, shall he live?

18:25 Is not my way equal?

18:25 Are not your ways unequal?

18:29 Are not my ways equal?

18:29 Are not your ways unequal?

18:31 Why will ye die, O house of Israel?

19:2 What is thy mother?

20:3 Are ye come to enquire of me?

20:4 Wilt thou judge them, son of man, wilt thou judge them?

20:29 What is the high place whereunto ye go?

20:30 Are ye polluted after the manner of your fathers?

20:30 Commit ye whoredom after their abominations?

20:31 Shall I be enquired of by you, O house of Israel?

20:49 Doth he not speak parables?

21:7 Wherefore sighest thou?

21:10 Should we then make mirth?

21:13 What if the sword contemn even the rod?

21:30 Shall I cause it to return into his sheath?

22:2 Wilt thou judge, wilt thou judge the bloody city? yea, thou shalt shew her all her abomination.

22:14 Can thine heart endure, or can thine hands be strong, in the days that I shall deal with thee?

23:36 Wilt thou judge Aholah and Aholibah?

23:43 Will they now commit whoredoms with her, and she with them?

24:19 Wilt thou not tell us what these things are to us, that thou doest so?

24:25, 26 Shall it not be in the day when I take from them their strength, the joy of their glory, the desire of their eyes, and that whereupon they set their minds, their sons and their daughters, That he that escapeth in that day shall come unto thee, to cause thee to hear it with thine ears?

26:15 Shall not the isles shake at the sound of thy fall, when the wounded cry, when the slaughter is made in the midst of thee?

27:32 What city is like Tyrus, like the destroyed in the midst of the sea?

28:9 Wilt thou yet say before him that slayeth thee, I am God?

31:2 Whom art thou like in thy greatness?

31:18 To whom art thou thus like in glory and in greatness among the trees of Eden?

32:19 Whom dost thou pass in beauty?

33:10 If our transgressions and our sins be upon us, and we pine away in them, how should we then live?

33:11 Why will ye die, O house of Israel?

33:25 Shall ye possess the land?

33:26 Shall ye possess the land?

34:2 Should not the shepherds feed the flocks?

34:18 Seemeth it a small thing unto you to have eaten up the good pasture, but ye must tread down with your feet the residue of your pastures?

34:18 And to have drunk of the deep waters, but ye must foul the residue with your feet?

37:3 Can these bones live?

37:18 Wilt thou not shew us what thou meanest by these?

38:13 Art thou come to take a spoil?

38:13 Hast thou gathered thy company to take a prey?

38:13 To carry away silver and gold, to take away cattle and goods, to take a great spoil?

38:14 When my people of Israel dwelleth safely, shalt thou not know it?

38:17 Art thou he of whom I have spoken in old time by my servants the prophets of Israel, which prophesied in those days many years that I would bring thee against them?

47:6 Hast thou seen this?

The Book of
Daniel

1:10 Why should he see your faces worse liking than the children which are of your sort?

2:15 Why is the decree so hasty from the king?

2:26 Art thou able to make known unto me the dream which I have seen, and the interpretation thereof?

3:14 Is it true, O Shadrach, Meshach, and Abednego, do not ye serve my gods, nor worship the golden image which I have set up?

3:15 Who is that God that shall deliver you out of my hands?

3:24 Did not we cast three men bound into the midst of the fire?

4:30 Is not this great Babylon, that I have built for the house of the kingdom by the might of my power, and for the honour of my majesty?

4:35 What doest thou?

5:13 Art thou that Daniel, which art of the children of the captivity of Judah, whom the king my father brought out of Jewry?

6:12 Hast thou not signed a decree, that every man that shall ask a petition of any God or man within thirty days, save of thee, O king, shall be cast into the den of lions?

6:20 Is thy God, whom thou servest continually, able to deliver thee from the lions?

8:13 How long shall be the vision concerning the daily sacrifice, and the transgression of desolation, to give both the sanctuary and the host to be trodden under foot?

10:17 How can the servant of this my lord talk with this my lord?

10:20 Knowest thou wherefore I come unto thee?

12:6 How long shall it be to the end of these wonders?

12:8 What shall be the end of these things?

MINOR PROPHETS

What wilt thou give?
Hosea 9:14

The Book of
Hosea

6:4 What shall I do unto thee?*

6:4 What shall I do unto thee?**

8:5 How long will it be ere they attain to innocency?

9:5 What will ye do in the solemn day, and in the day of the feast of the LORD?

9:14 What wilt thou give?

10:3 What then should a king do to us?

11:8 How shall I give thee up, Ephraim?

11:8 How shall I deliver thee, Israel?

11:8 How shall I make thee as Admah?

11:8 How shall I set thee as Zeboim?

12:11 Is there iniquity in Gilead?

13:10 Where is any other that may save thee in all thy cities?

13:10 And thy judges of whom thou saidst, Give me a king and princes?

14:8 What have I to do any more with idols?

14:9 Who is wise, and he shall understand these things?

14:9 Prudent, and he shall know them?

The Book of
Joel

1:2 Hath this been in your days, or even in the days of your fathers?

1:16 Is not the meat cut off before our eyes, yea, joy and gladness from the house of our God?

2:11 Who can abide it?

2:14 Who knoweth if he will return and repent, and leave a blessing behind him; even a meat offering and a drink offering unto the LORD your God?

2:17 Wherefore should they say among the people, Where is their God?

3:4 What have ye to do with me, O Tyre, and Zidon, and all the coasts of Palestine?

3:4 Will ye render me a recompence?

The Book of
Amos

2:11 Is it not even thus, O ye children of Israel?

3:3 Can two walk together, except they be agreed?

3:4 Will a lion roar in the forest, when he hath no prey?

3:4 Will a young lion cry out of his den, if he have taken nothing?

3:5 Can a bird fall in a snare upon the earth, where no gin is for him?

3:5 Shall one take up a snare from the earth, and have taken nothing at all?

3:6 Shall a trumpet be blown in the city, and the people not be afraid?

3:6 Shall there be evil in a city, and the LORD hath not done it?

3:8 Who will not fear?

3:8 Who can but prophesy?

5:18 To what end is it for you?

5:20 Shall not the day of the LORD be darkness, and not light?

5:20 Even very dark, and no brightness in it?

5:25 Have ye offered unto me sacrifices and offerings in the wilderness forty years, O house of Israel?

6:2 Be they better than these kingdoms?

6:2 Or their border greater than your border?

6:10 Is there yet any with thee?

6:12 Shall horses run upon the rock?

6:12 Will one plow there with oxen?

6:13 Have we not taken to us horns by our own strength?

7:2 By whom shall Jacob arise?

7:8 What seest thou?

8:2 What seest thou?

8:5 When will the new moon be gone, that we may sell corn?

8:5 And the sabbath, that we may set forth wheat, making the ephah small, and the shekel great, and falsifying the balances by deceit?

8:6 And sell the refuse of the wheat?

8:8 Shall not the land tremble for this, and every one mourn that dwelleth therein?

9:7 Are ye not as children of the Ethiopians unto me, O children of Israel?

9:7 Have not I brought up Israel out of the land of Egypt?

9:7 And the Philistines from Caphtor, and the Syrians from Kir?

The Book of
Obadiah

1:3 Who shall bring me down to the ground?

1:5 If thieves came to thee, if robbers by night, (how art thou cut off!) would they not have stolen till they had enough?

1:5 If the grape gatherers came to thee, would they not leave some grapes?

1:8 Shall I not in that day, saith the LORD, even destroy the wisemen out of Edom, and understanding out of the mount of Esau?

The Book of
Jonah

1:6 What meanest thou, O sleeper?

1:8 What is thine occupation?

1:8 And whence comest thou?

1:8 What is thy country?

1:8 And of what people art thou?

1:10 Why hast thou done this?

1:11 What shall we do unto thee, that the sea may be calm unto us?

3:9 Who can tell if God will turn and repent, and turn away from his fierce anger, that we perish not?

4:2 Was not this my saying, when I was yet in my country?

4:4 Doest thou well to be angry?

4:9 Doest thou well to be angry for the gourd?

4:11 Should not I spare Nineveh, that great city, wherein are more than sixscore thousand persons that cannot discern between their right hand and their left hand; and also much cattle?

The Book of
Micah

1:5 What is the transgression of Jacob?

1:5 Is it not Samaria?

1:5 What are the high places of Judah?

1:5 Are they not Jerusalem?

2:7 Is the spirit of the LORD straitened?

2:7 Are these his doings?

2:7 Do not my words do good to him that walketh uprightly?

3:1 Is it not for you to know judgment?

4:9 Why dost thou cry out aloud?

4:9 Is there no king in thee?

4:9 Is thy counsellor perished?

6:3 What have I done unto thee?

6:3 Wherein have I wearied thee?

6:6 Wherewith shall I come before the LORD, and bow myself before the high God?

6:6 Shall I come before him with burnt offerings, with calves of a year old?

6:7 Will the LORD be pleased with thousands of rams, or with ten thousands of rivers of oil?

6:7 Shall I give my firstborn for my transgression, the fruit of my body for the sin of my soul?

6:8 What doth the LORD require of thee, but to do justly, and to love mercy, and to walk humbly with thy God?

6:10 Are there yet the treasures of wickedness in the house of the wicked, and the scant measure that is abominable?

6:11 Shall I count them pure with the wicked balances, and with the bag of deceitful weights?

7:10 Where is the LORD thy God?

7:18 Who is a God like unto thee, that pardoneth iniquity, and passeth by the transgression of the remnant of his heritage?

The Book of
Nahum

1:6 Who can stand before his indignation?

1:6 Who can abide in the fierceness of his anger?

1:9 What do ye imagine against the LORD?

2:11 Where is the dwelling of the lions, and the feeding place of the young lions, where the lion, even the old lion, walked, and the lion's whelp, and none made them afraid?

3:7 Who will bemoan her?

3:7 Whence shall I seek comforters for thee?

3:8 Art thou better than populous No, that was situate among the rivers, that had the waters round about it, whose rampart was the sea, and her wall was from the sea?

3:19 Upon whom hath not thy wickedness passed continually?

The Book of
Habakkuk

1:3 Why dost thou shew me iniquity, and cause me to behold grievance?

1:12 Art thou not from everlasting, O LORD my God, mine Holy One?

1:13 Wherefore lookest thou upon them that deal treacherously, and holdest thy tongue when the wicked devoureth the man that is more righteous than he?

1:14 And makest men as the fishes of the sea, as the creeping things, that have no ruler over them?

1:17 Shall they therefore empty their net, and not spare continually to slay the nations?

2:6 How long?

2:7 Shall they not rise up suddenly that shall bite thee, and awake that shall vex thee, and thou shalt be for booties unto them?

2:13 Is it not of the LORD of hosts that the people shall labour in the very fire, and the people shall weary themselves for very vanity?

2:18 What profiteth the graven image that the maker thereof hath graven it; the molten image, and a teacher of lies, that the maker of his work trusteth therein, to make dumb idols?

3:8 Was the LORD displeased against the rivers?

3:8 Was thine anger against the rivers?

3:8 Was thy wrath against the sea, that thou didst ride upon thine horses and thy chariots of salvation?

The Book of
Zephaniah

No question is asked in the book of Zephaniah.

The Book of
Haggai

1:4 Is it time for you, O ye, to dwell in your cieled houses, and this house lie waste?

1:9 Ye looked for much, and, lo, it came to little; and when ye brought it home, I did blow upon it. Why? saith the LORD of hosts. Because of mine house that is waste, and ye run every man unto his own house.

2:3 Who is left among you that saw this house in her first glory?

2:3 How do ye see it now?

2:3 Is it not in your eyes in comparison of it as nothing?

2:12 If one bear holy flesh in the skirt of his garment, and with his skirt do touch bread, or pottage, or wine, or oil, or any meat, shall it be holy?

2:13 If one that is unclean by a dead body touch any of these, shall it be unclean?

2:19 Is the seed yet in the barn?

The Book of
Zechariah

1:5 Where are they?

1:5 Do they live for ever?

1:6 Did they not take hold of your fathers?

1:9 What are these?

1:12 How long wilt thou not have mercy on Jerusalem and on the cities of Judah, against which thou hast had indignation these threescore and ten years?

1:19 What be these?

1:21 What come these to do?

2:2 Whither goest thou?

3:2 Is not this a brand plucked out of the fire?

4:2 What seest thou?

4:4 What are these, my lord?

4:5 Knowest thou not what these be?

4:7 Who art thou, O great mountain?

4:11 What are these two olive trees upon the right side of the candlestick and upon the left side thereof?

4:12 What be these two olive branches which through the two golden pipes empty the golden oil out of themselves?

4:13 Knowest thou not what these be?

5:2 What seest thou?

5:6 What is it?

5:10 Whither do these bear the ephah?

6:4 What are these, my lord?

7:3 Should I weep in the fifth month, separating myself, as I have done these so many years?

7:5 When ye fasted and mourned in the fifth and seventh month, even those seventy years, did ye at all fast unto me, even to me?

7:6 When ye did eat, and when ye did drink, did not ye eat for yourselves, and drink for yourselves?

7:7 Should ye not hear the words which the LORD hath cried by the former prophets, when Jerusalem was inhabited and in prosperity, and the cities thereof round about her, when men inhabited the south and the plain?

8:6 If it be marvellous in the eyes of the remnant of this people in these days, should it also be marvellous in mine eyes?

13:6 What are these wounds in thine hands?

The Book of
Malachi

1:2 Wherein hast thou loved us?

1:2 Was not Esau Jacob's brother?

1:6 Where is mine honour?

1:6 Where is my fear?

1:6 Wherein have we despised thy name?

1:8 Is it not evil?

1:8 Will he be pleased with thee, or accept thy person?

1:9 Will he regard your persons?

1:10 Who is there even among you that would shut the doors for nought?

1:13 Ye brought an offering: should I accept this of your hand? saith the LORD.

2:10 Have we not all one father?

2:10 Hath not one God created us?

2:10 Why do we deal treacherously every man against his brother, by profaning the covenant of our fathers?

2:14 Wherefore?

2:15 Did not he make one?

2:15 And wherefore one?

2:17 Wherein have we wearied him?

2:17 Where is the God of judgment?

3:2 Who may abide the day of his coming?

3:2 Who shall stand when he appeareth?

3:7 Return unto me, and I will return unto you, saith the LORD of hosts. But ye said, Wherein shall we return?

3:8 Will a man rob God?

3:8 Wherein have we robbed thee?

3:13 What have we spoken so much against thee?

3:14 What profit is it that we have kept his ordinance, and that we have walked mournfully before the LORD of hosts?

THE GOSPELS

Art thou he that should come, or do we look for another?
Matthew 11:3

The Gospel according to
Matthew

2:2 Where is he that is born King of the Jews?

3:7 Who hath warned you to flee from the wrath to come?

3:14 Comest thou to me?

5:13 If the salt have lost his savour, wherewith shall it be salted?

5:46 If ye love them which love you, what reward have ye?

5:46 Do not even the publicans the same?

5:47 If ye salute your brethren only, what do ye more than others?

5:47 Do not even the publicans so?

6:25 Is not the life more than meat, and the body than raiment?

6:26 Are ye not much better than they?

6:27 Which of you by taking thought can add one cubit unto his stature?

6:28 Why take ye thought for raiment?

6:30 If God so clothe the grass of the field, which to day is, and to morrow is cast into the oven, shall he not much more clothe you, O ye of little faith?

6:31 What shall we eat?

6:31 What shall we drink?

6:31 Wherewithal shall we be clothed?

7:3 Why beholdest thou the mote that is in thy brother's eye, but considerest not the beam that is in thine own eye?

7:4 How wilt thou say to thy brother, Let me pull out the mote out of thine eye; and, behold, a beam is in thine own eye?

7:9 What man is there of you, whom if his son ask bread, will he give him a stone?

7:10 Or if he ask a fish, will he give him a serpent?

7:11 If ye then, being evil, know how to give good gifts unto your children, how much more shall your Father which is in heaven give good things to them that ask him?

7:16 Do men gather grapes of thorns, or figs of thistles?

7:22 Lord, Lord, have we not prophesied in thy name?

7:22 And in thy name have cast out devils?

7:22 And in thy name done many wonderful works?

8:26 Why are ye fearful, O ye of little faith?

8:29 What have we to do with thee, Jesus, thou Son of God?

8:29 Art thou come hither to torment us before the time?

9:4 Wherefore think ye evil in your hearts?

9:5 Whether is easier, to say, Thy sins be forgiven thee; or to say, Arise, and walk?

9:11 Why eateth your Master with publicans and sinners?

9:14 Why do we and the Pharisees fast oft, but thy disciples fast not?

9:15 Can the children of the bridechamber mourn, as long as the bridegroom is with them?

9:28 Believe ye that I am able to do this?

10:25 If they have called the master of the house Beelzebub, how much more shall they call them of his household?

10:29 Are not two sparrows sold for a farthing?

11:3 Art thou he that should come, or do we look for another?

11:7 What went ye out into the wilderness to see?

11:7 A reed shaken with the wind?

11:8 But what went ye out for to see?

11:8 A man clothed in soft raiment?

11:9 But what went ye out for to see?

11:9 A prophet?

11:16 Whereunto shall I liken this generation?

12:3, 4 How can ye, being evil, speak good things?

12:5 Or have ye not read in the law, how that on the sabbath days the priests in the temple profane the sabbath, and are blameless?

12:10 Is it lawful to heal on the sabbath days? that they might accuse him.

12:11 What man shall there be among you, that shall have one sheep, and if it fall into a pit on the sabbath day, will he not lay hold on it, and lift it out?

12:12 How much then is a man better than a sheep?

12:23 Is not this the son of David?

12:26 If Satan cast out Satan, he is divided against himself; how shall then his kingdom stand?

12:27 And if I by Beelzebub cast out devils, by whom do your children cast them out?

12:29 How can one enter into a strong man's house, and spoil his goods, except he first bind the strong man? and then he will spoil his house.

12:48 Who is my mother?

12:48 Who are my brethren?

12:3,4 Have ye not read what David did, when he was an hungred, and they that were with him; How he entered into the house of God, and did eat the shewbread, which was not lawful for him to eat, neither for them which were with him, but only for the priests?

13:10 Why speakest thou unto them in parables?

13:27 Didst not thou sow good seed in thy field?

13:27 From whence then hath it tares?

13:28 Wilt thou then that we go and gather them up?

13:51 Have ye understood all these things?

13:54 Whence hath this man this wisdom, and these mighty works?

13:55 Is not this the carpenter's son?

13:55 Is not his mother called Mary?

13:55 And his brethren, James, and Joses, and Simon, and Judas?

13:56 And his sisters, are they not all with us?

13:56 Whence then hath this man all these things?

14:31 Wherefore didst thou doubt?

15:2 Why do thy disciples transgress the tradition of the elders?

15:3 Why do ye also transgress the commandment of God by your tradition?

15:12 Knowest thou that the Pharisees were offended, after they heard this saying?

15:16 Are ye also yet without understanding?

15:17 Do not ye yet understand, that whatsoever entereth in at the mouth goeth into the belly, and is cast out into the draught?

15:33 Whence should we have so much bread in the wilderness, as to fill so great a multitude?

15:34 How many loaves have ye?

16:3 Can ye not discern the signs of the times?

16:8 Why reason ye among yourselves, because ye have brought no bread?

16:9 Do ye not yet understand, neither remember the five loaves of the five thousand, and how many baskets ye took up?

16:10 Neither the seven loaves of the four thousand, and how many baskets ye took up?

16:11 How is it that ye do not understand that I spake it not to you concerning bread, that ye should beware of the leaven of the Pharisees and of the Sadducees?

16:13 Whom do men say that I the Son of man am?

16:15 But whom say ye that I am?

16:26 For what is a man profited, if he shall gain the whole world, and lose his own soul?

16:26 or what shall a man give in exchange for his soul?

17:10 Why then say the scribes that Elias must first come?

17:17 How long shall I be with you?

17:17 How long shall I suffer you?

17:19 Why could not we cast him out?

17:24 Doth not your master pay tribute?

17:25 What thinkest thou, Simon?

17:25 Of whom do the kings of the earth take custom or tribute?

17:25 Of their own children, or of strangers?

18:1 Who is the greatest in the kingdom of heaven?

18:12 How think ye?

18:12 If a man have an hundred sheep, and one of them be gone astray, doth he not leave the ninety and nine, and goeth into the mountains, and seeketh that which is gone astray?

18:21 How oft shall my brother sin against me, and I forgive him?

18:21 Till seven times?

18:33 Shouldest not thou also have had compassion on thy fellowservant, even as I had pity on thee?

19:3 Is it lawful for a man to put away his wife for every cause?

19:4, 5 Have ye not read, that he which made them at the beginning made them male and female, And said, For this cause shall a man leave father and mother, and shall cleave to his wife: and they twain shall be one flesh?

19:7 Why did Moses then command to give a writing of divorcement, and to put her away?

19:16 Good Master, what good thing shall I do, that I may have eternal life?

19:17 Why callest thou me good?

19:18 Which?

19:20 What lack I yet?

19:25 Who then can be saved?

19:27 We have forsaken all, and followed thee; what shall we have therefore?

20:6 Why stand ye here all the day idle?

20:13 I do thee no wrong: didst not thou agree with me for a penny?

20:15 Is it not lawful for me to do what I will with mine own?

20:15 Is thine eye evil, because I am good?

20:21 What wilt thou?

20:22 Are ye able to drink of the cup that I shall drink of, and to be baptized with the baptism that I am baptized with?

20:32 What will ye that I shall do unto you?

21:10 Who is this?

21:16 Hearest thou what these say?

21:16 Have ye never read, Out of the mouth of babes and sucklings thou hast perfected praise?

21:23 By what authority doest thou these things?

21:23 And who gave thee this authority?

21:25 The baptism of John, whence was it?

21:25 From heaven, or of men?

21:25 If we shall say, From heaven; he will say unto us, Why did ye not then believe him?

21:28 What think ye?

21:31 Whether of them twain did the will of his father?

21:40 When the lord therefore of the vineyard cometh, what will he do unto those husbandmen?

21:42 Did ye never read in the scriptures, The stone which the builders rejected, the same is become the head of the corner: this is the Lord's doing, and it is marvellous in our eyes?

22:12 Friend, how camest thou in hither not having a wedding garment?

22:17 What thinkest thou?

22:17 Is it lawful to give tribute unto Caesar, or not?

22:18 Why tempt ye me, ye hypocrites?

22:20 Whose is this image and superscription?

22:28 Therefore in the resurrection whose wife shall she be of the seven?

22:32 Have ye not read that which was spoken unto you by God, saying, I am the God of Abraham, and the God of Isaac, and the God of Jacob? God is not the God of the dead, but of the living.

22:36 Master, which is the great commandment in the law?

22:42 What think ye of Christ?

22:42 Whose son is he?

22:43, 44 How then doth David in spirit call him Lord, saying, The LORD said unto my Lord, Sit thou on my right hand, till I make thine enemies thy footstool?

22:45 If David then call him Lord, how is he his son?

23:17 Whether is greater, the gold, or the temple that sanctifieth the gold?

23:19 Whether is greater, the gift, or the altar that sanctifieth the gift?

23:33 How can ye escape the damnation of hell?

24:2 See ye not all these things?

24:3 When shall these things be?

24:3 And what shall be the sign of thy coming, and of the end of the world?

24:25 Who then is a faithful and wise servant, whom his lord hath made ruler over his household, to give them meat in due season?

25:37 Lord, when saw we thee an hungred, and fed thee?

25:37 Or thirsty, and gave thee drink?

25:38 When saw we thee a stranger, and took thee in?

25:38 Or naked, and clothed thee?

25:39 Or when saw we thee sick, or in prison, and came unto thee?

25:44 Lord, when saw we thee an hungred, or athirst, or a stranger, or naked, or sick, or in prison, and did not minister unto thee?

26:8 To what purpose is this waste?

26:10 Why trouble ye the woman?

26:15 What will ye give me, and I will deliver him unto you?

26:17 Where wilt thou that we prepare for thee to eat the passover?

26:22 Lord, is it I?

26:25 Master, is it I?

26:40 What, could ye not watch with me one hour?

26:50 Friend, wherefore art thou come?

26:53 Thinkest thou that I cannot now pray to my Father, and he shall presently give me more than twelve legions of angels?

26:54 But how then shall the scriptures be fulfilled, that thus it must be?

26:55 Are ye come out as against a thief with swords and staves for to take me?

26:62 Answerest thou nothing?

26:62 What is it which these witness against thee?

26:65 What further need have we of witnesses?

26:66 What think ye?

26:68 Who is he that smote thee?

27:4 What is that to us?

27:11 Art thou the King of the Jews?

27:13 Hearest thou not how many things they witness against thee?

27:17 Whom will ye that I release unto you?

27:17 Barabbas, or Jesus which is called Christ?

27:21 Whether of the twain will ye that I release unto you?

27:22 What shall I do then with Jesus which is called Christ?

27:23 Why, what evil hath he done?

27:46 Eli, Eli, lama sabachthani?

27:46 My God, my God, why hast thou forsaken me?

The Gospel according to
Mark

1:24 What have we to do with thee, thou Jesus of Nazareth?

1:24 Art thou come to destroy us?

1:27 What thing is this?

1:27 What new doctrine is this?

2:7 Why doth this man thus speak blasphemies?

2:7 Who can forgive sins but God only?

2:8 Why reason ye these things in your hearts?

2:9 Whether is it easier to say to the sick of the palsy, Thy sins be forgiven thee; or to say, Arise, and take up thy bed, and walk?

2:16 How is it that he eateth and drinketh with publicans and sinners?

2:18 Why do the disciples of John and of the Pharisees fast, but thy disciples fast not?

2:19 Can the children of the bridechamber fast, while the bridegroom is with them?

2:24 Why do they on the sabbath day that which is not lawful?

2:25 Have ye never read what David did, when he had need, and was an hungred, he, and they that were with him?

2:26 How he went into the house of God in the days of Abiathar the high priest, and did eat the shewbread, which is not lawful to eat but for the priests, and gave also to them which were with him?

3:4 Is it lawful to do good on the sabbath days, or to do evil?

3:4 To save life, or to kill?

3:23 How can Satan cast out Satan?

3:33 Who is my mother, or my brethren?

4:13 Know ye not this parable?

4:13 And how then will ye know all parables?

4:21 Is a candle brought to be put under a bushel, or under a bed?

4:21 And not to be set on a candlestick?

4:30 Whereunto shall we liken the kingdom of God?

4:30 Or with what comparison shall we compare it?

4:38 Master, carest thou not that we perish?

4:40 Why are ye so fearful?

4:40 How is it that ye have no faith?

4:41 What manner of man is this, that even the wind and the sea obey him?

5:7 What have I to do with thee, Jesus, thou Son of the most high God?

5:9 What is thy name?

5:30 Who touched my clothes?

5:31 Who touched me?

5:35 Why troublest thou the Master any further?

5:39 Why make ye this ado, and weep?

6:2 From whence hath this man these things?

6:2 And what wisdom is this which is given unto him, that even such mighty works are wrought by his hands?

6:3 Is not this the carpenter, the son of Mary, the brother of James, and Joses, and of Juda, and Simon?

6:3 And are not his sisters here with us?

6:24 What shall I ask?

6:37 Shall we go and buy two hundred pennyworth of bread, and give them to eat?

6:38 How many loaves have ye?

7:5 Why walk not thy disciples according to the tradition of the elders, but eat bread with unwashen hands?

7:18 Are ye so without understanding also?

7:18,19 Do ye not perceive, that whatsoever thing from without entereth into the man, it cannot defile him; Because it entereth not into his heart, but into the belly, and goeth out into the draught, purging all meats?

8:4 From whence can a man satisfy these men with bread here in the wilderness?

8:5 How many loaves have ye?

8:12 Why doth this generation seek after a sign?

8:17 Why reason ye, because ye have no bread?

8:17 Perceive ye not yet, neither understand?

8:17 Have ye your heart yet hardened?

8:18 Having eyes, see ye not?

8:18 And having ears, hear ye not?

8:18 And do ye not remember?

8:19 When I brake the five loaves among five thousand, how many baskets full of fragments took ye up?

8:20 And when the seven among four thousand, how many baskets full of fragments took ye up?

8:21 How is it that ye do not understand?

8:27 Whom do men say that I am?

8:29 But whom say ye that I am?

8:37 For what shall it profit a man, if he shall gain the whole world, and lose his own soul?

8:37 Or what shall a man give in exchange for his soul?

9:11 Why say the scribes that Elias must first come?

9:16 What question ye with them?

9:19 O faithless generation, how long shall I be with you?

9:19 How long shall I suffer you?

9:21 How long is it ago since this came unto him?

9:28 Why could not we cast him out?

9:33 What was it that ye disputed among yourselves by the way?

9:50 Salt is good: but if the salt have lost his saltness, wherewith will ye season it?

10:2 Is it lawful for a man to put away his wife?

10:3 What did Moses command you?

10:17 Good Master, what shall I do that I may inherit eternal life?

10:18 Why callest thou me good?

10:26 Who then can be saved?

10:36 What would ye that I should do for you?

10:38 Ye know not what ye ask: can ye drink of the cup that I drink of?

10:38 And be baptized with the baptism that I am baptized with?

10:51 What wilt thou that I should do unto thee?

11:3 Why do ye this?

11:5 What do ye, loosing the colt?

11:17 Is it not written, My house shall be called of all nations the house of prayer?

11:28 By what authority doest thou these things?

11:28 And who gave thee this authority to do these things?

11:30 The baptism of John, was it from heaven, or of men?

11:31 If we shall say, From heaven; he will say, Why then did ye not believe him?

12:9 What shall therefore the lord of the vineyard do?

12:11 Have ye not read this scripture; The stone which the builders rejected is become the head of the corner: This was the Lord's doing, and it is marvellous in our eyes?

12:14 Is it lawful to give tribute to Caesar, or not?

12:15 Shall we give, or shall we not give?

12:15 Why tempt ye me?

12:16 Whose is this image and superscription?

12:20, 21, 22, 23 there were seven brethren: and the first took a wife, and dying left no seed. And the second took her, and died, neither left he any seed: and the third likewise. And the seven had her, and left no seed: last of all the woman died also. In the resurrection therefore, when they shall rise, whose wife shall she be of them?

12:24 Do ye not therefore err, because ye know not the scriptures, neither the power of God?

12:26 Have ye not read in the book of Moses, how in the bush God spake unto him, saying, I am the God of Abraham, and the God of Isaac, and the God of Jacob?

12:28 Which is the first commandment of all?

12:35 How say the scribes that Christ is the Son of David?

12:37 David therefore himself calleth him Lord; and whence is he then his son?

13:2 Seest thou these great buildings?

13:4 Tell us, when shall these things be?

13:4 And what shall be the sign when all these things shall be fulfilled?

14:4 Why was this waste of the ointment made?

14:6 Let her alone; why trouble ye her?

14:12 Where wilt thou that we go and prepare that thou mayest eat the passover?

14:14 The Master saith, Where is the guest chamber, where I shall eat the passover with my disciples?

14:18, 19 As they sat and did eat, Jesus said, Verily I say unto you, One of you which eateth with me shall betray me. And they began to be sorrowful, and to say unto him one by one, Is it I?

14:19 And another said, Is it I?

14:37 He cometh, and findeth them sleeping, and saith unto Peter, Simon, sleepest thou?

14:37 Couldest not thou watch one hour?

14:48 Are ye come out, as against a thief, with swords and with staves to take me?

14:60 Answerest thou nothing?

14:60 What is it which these witness against thee?

14:61 Art thou the Christ, the Son of the Blessed?

14:63 What need we any further witnesses?

14:64 What think ye?

15:2 Art thou the King of the Jews?

15:4 Answerest thou nothing?

15:9 Will ye that I release unto you the King of the Jews?

15:12 What will ye then that I shall do unto him whom ye call the King of the Jews?

15:14 Why, what evil hath he done?

15:34 Eloi, Eloi, lama sabachthani?

15:34 My God, my God, why hast thou forsaken me?

16:3 Who shall roll us away the stone from the door of the sepulchre?

The Gospel according to
Luke

1:18 Whereby shall I know this?

1:34 How shall this be, seeing I know not a man?

1:43 Whence is this to me, that the mother of my Lord should come to me?

2:48 Son, why hast thou thus dealt with us?

2:49 How is it that ye sought me?

2:49 Wist ye not that I must be about my Father's business?

3:7 O generation of vipers, who hath warned you to flee from the wrath to come?

3:10 What shall we do then?

3:12 Master, what shall we do?

3:14 What shall we do?

4:22 Is not this Joseph's son?

4:34 What have we to do with thee, thou Jesus of Nazareth?

4:34 Art thou come to destroy us?

5:21 Who is this which speaketh blasphemies?

5:21 Who can forgive sins, but God alone?

5:22 What reason ye in your hearts?

5:23 Whether is easier, to say, Thy sins be forgiven thee; or to say, Rise up and walk?

5:30 Why do ye eat and drink with publicans and sinners?

5:33 Why do the disciples of John fast often, and make prayers, and likewise the disciples of the Pharisees; but thine eat and drink?

5:34 Can ye make the children of the bridechamber fast, while the bridegroom is with them?

6:2 Why do ye that which is not lawful to do on the sabbath days?

6:3,4 Have ye not read so much as this, what David did, when himself was an hungred, and they which were with him; How he went into the house of God, and did take and eat the shewbread, and gave also to them that were with him; which it is not lawful to eat but for the priests alone?

6:9 Is it lawful on the sabbath days to do good, or to do evil?

6:9 To save life, or to destroy it?

6:32 For if ye love them which love you, what thank have ye?

6:33 And if ye do good to them which do good to you, what thank have ye?

6:34 And if ye lend to them of whom ye hope to receive, what thank have ye?

6:39 Can the blind lead the blind?

6:39 Shall they not both fall into the ditch?

6:41 Why beholdest thou the mote that is in thy brother's eye, but perceivest not the beam that is in thine own eye?

6:42 How canst thou say to thy brother, Brother, let me pull out the mote that is in thine eye, when thou thyself beholdest not the beam that is in thine own eye?

6:46 Why call ye me, Lord, Lord, and do not the things which I say?

7:19 Art thou he that should come?

7:19 Or look we for another?

7:20 Art thou he that should come?

7:20 Or look we for another?

7:24 What went ye out into the wilderness for to see?

7:24 A reed shaken with the wind?

7:25 But what went ye out for to see?

7:25 A man clothed in soft raiment?

7:26 But what went ye out for to see?

7:26 A prophet?

7:31 Whereunto then shall I liken the men of this generation?

7:31 And to what are they like?

7:42 Which of them will love him most?

7:44 Seest thou this woman?

7:49 Who is this that forgiveth sins also?

8:9 What might this parable be?

8:25 Where is your faith?

8:28 What have I to do with thee, Jesus, thou Son of God most high?

8:30 What is thy name?

8:45 Who touched me?

8:45 Master, the multitude throng thee and press thee, and sayest thou, Who touched me?

9:9 Who is this, of whom I hear such things?

9:18 Whom say the people that I am?

9:20 But whom say ye that I am?

9:25 For what is a man advantaged, if he gain the whole world, and lose himself, or be cast away?

9:41 How long shall I be with you, and suffer you?

9:54 Wilt thou that we command fire to come down from heaven, and consume them, even as Elias did?

10:25 Master, what shall I do to inherit eternal life?

10:26 What is written in the law?

10:26 How readest thou?

10:29 Who is my neighbour?

10:36 Which now of these three, thinkest thou, was neighbour unto him that fell among the thieves?

10:40 Dost thou not care that my sister hath left me to serve alone?

11:6 Which of you shall have a friend, and shall go unto him at midnight, and say unto him, Friend, lend me three loaves; For a friend of mine in his journey is come to me, and I have nothing to set before him?

11:11 If a son shall ask bread of any of you that is a father, will he give him a stone?

11:11 Or if he ask a fish, will he for a fish give him a serpent?

11:12 Or if he shall ask an egg, will he offer him a scorpion?

11:13 If ye then, being evil, know how to give good gifts unto your children: how much more shall your heavenly Father give the Holy Spirit to them that ask him?

11:18 If Satan also be divided against himself, how shall his kingdom stand?

11:19 And if I by Beelzebub cast out devils, by whom do your sons cast them out?

11:40 Did not he that made that which is without make that which is within also?

12:6 Are not five sparrows sold for two farthings, and not one of them is forgotten before God?

12:14 Man, who made me a judge or a divider over you?

12:17 What shall I do, because I have no room where to bestow my fruits?

12:20 Whose shall those things be, which thou hast provided?

12:24 How much more are ye better than the fowls?

12:25 Which of you with taking thought can add to his stature one cubit?

12:26 If ye then be not able to do that thing which is least, why take ye thought for the rest?

12:28 If then God so clothe the grass, which is to day in the field, and to morrow is cast into the oven; how much more will he clothe you, O ye of little faith?

12:41 Speakest thou this parable unto us, or even to all?

12:42 Who then is that faithful and wise steward, whom his lord shall make ruler over his household, to give them their portion of meat in due season?

12:49 I am come to send fire on the earth; and what will I, if it be already kindled?

12:51 Suppose ye that I am come to give peace on earth?

12:56 How is it that ye do not discern this time?

12:57 Yea, and why even of yourselves judge ye not what is right?

13:2 Suppose ye that these Galilaeans were sinners above all the Galilaeans, because they suffered such things?

13:4 Or those eighteen, upon whom the tower in Siloam fell, and slew them, think ye that they were sinners above all men that dwelt in Jerusalem?

13:7 Why cumbereth it the ground?

13:15 Doth not each one of you on the sabbath loose his ox or his ass from the stall, and lead him away to watering?

13:16 And ought not this woman, being a daughter of Abraham, whom Satan hath bound, lo, these eighteen years, be loosed from this bond on the sabbath day?

13:18 Unto what is the kingdom of God like?

13:18 And whereunto shall I resemble it?

13:20 Whereunto shall I liken the kingdom of God?

13:23 Lord, are there few that be saved?

14:3 Is it lawful to heal on the sabbath day?

14:5 Which of you shall have an ass or an ox fallen into a pit, and will not straightway pull him out on the sabbath day?

14:28 For which of you, intending to build a tower, sitteth not down first, and counteth the cost, whether he have sufficient to finish it?

14:31 What king, going to make war against another king, sitteth not down first, and consulteth whether he be able with ten thousand to meet him that cometh against him with twenty thousand?

14:34 If the salt have lost his savour, wherewith shall it be seasoned?

15:4 What man of you, having an hundred sheep, if he lose one of them, doth not leave the ninety and nine in the wilderness, and go after that which is lost, until he find it?

15:8 Either what woman having ten pieces of silver, if she lose one piece, doth not light a candle, and sweep the house, and seek diligently till she find it?

16:2 How is it that I hear this of thee?

16:3 What shall I do?

16:5 How much owest thou unto my lord?

16:7 And how much owest thou?

16:11 If therefore ye have not been faithful in the unrighteous mammon, who will commit to your trust the true riches?

16:12 And if ye have not been faithful in that which is another man's, who shall give you that which is your own?

17:7 Which of you, having a servant plowing or feeding cattle, will say unto him by and by, when he is come from the field, Go and sit down to meat?

17:8 And will not rather say unto him, Make ready wherewith I may sup, and gird thyself, and serve me, till I have eaten and drunken; and afterward thou shalt eat and drink?

17:9 Doth he thank that servant because he did the things that were commanded him?

17:17 Were there not ten cleansed?

17:17 But where are the nine?

17:37 Where, Lord?

18:7 Shall not God avenge his own elect, which cry day and night unto him, though he bear long with them?

18:8 When the Son of man cometh, shall he find faith on the earth?

18:18 Good Master, what shall I do to inherit eternal life?

18:19 Why callest thou me good?

18:26 Who then can be saved?

18:41 What wilt thou that I shall do unto thee?

19:23 Wherefore then gavest not thou my money into the bank, that at my coming I might have required mine own with usury?

19:31 Why do ye loose him?

19:33 Why loose ye the colt?

20:2 Tell us, by what authority doest thou these things?

20:2 Or who is he that gave thee this authority?

20:4 The baptism of John, was it from heaven, or of men?

20:5 If we shall say, From heaven; he will say, Why then believed ye him not?

20:13 What shall I do?

20:15 What therefore shall the lord of the vineyard do unto them?

20:17 What is this then that is written, The stone which the builders rejected, the same is become the head of the corner?

20:22 Is it lawful for us to give tribute unto Caesar, or no?

20:23 Why tempt ye me?

20:24 Whose image and superscription hath it?

20:41 How say they that Christ is David's son?

20:44 How is he then his son?

20:28, 29, 30, 31, 32, 33 Master, Moses wrote unto us, If any man's brother die, having a wife, and he die without children, that his brother should take his wife, and raise up seed unto his brother. There were therefore seven brethren: and the first took a wife, and died without children. And the second took her to wife, and he died childless. And the third took her; and in like manner the seven also: and they left no children, and died. Last of all the woman died also. Therefore in the resurrection whose wife of them is she? For seven had her to wife.

21:7 When shall these things be?

21:7 And what sign will there be when these things shall come to pass?

22:9 Where wilt thou that we prepare?

22:11 Where is the guest chamber, where I shall eat the passover with my disciples?

22:27 For whether is greater, he that sitteth at meat, or he that serveth?

22:27 Is not he that sitteth at meat?

22:35 When I sent you without purse, and scrip, and shoes, lacked ye any thing?

22:46 Why sleep ye?

22:48 Betrayest thou the Son of man with a kiss?

22:49 Lord, shall we smite with the sword?

22:52 Be ye come out, as against a thief, with swords and staves?

22:64 Prophesy, who is it that smote thee?

22:67 Art thou the Christ?

22:71 What need we any further witness?

23:3 Art thou the King of the Jews?

23:22 Why, what evil hath he done?

23:31 If they do these things in a green tree, what shall be done in the dry?

23:40 Dost not thou fear God, seeing thou art in the same condemnation?

24:5 Why seek ye the living among the dead?

24:17 What manner of communications are these that ye have one to another, as ye walk, and are sad?

24:18 Art thou only a stranger in Jerusalem, and hast not known the things which are come to pass there in these days?

24:19 What things?

24:26 Ought not Christ to have suffered these things, and to enter into his glory?

24:32 Did not our heart burn within us, while he talked with us by the way, and while he opened to us the scriptures?

24:38 Why are ye troubled?

24:38 And why do thoughts arise in your hearts?

24:41 Have ye here any meat?

The Gospel according to
John

1:19 Who art thou?

1:21 What then?

1:21 Art thou Elias?

1:21 Art thou that prophet?

1:22 Who art thou?

1:22 What sayest thou of thyself?

1:25 Why baptizest thou then, if thou be not that Christ, nor Elias, neither that prophet?

1:38 What seek ye?

1:38 Rabbi, (which is to say, being interpreted, Master,) where dwellest thou?

1:46 Can there any good thing come out of Nazareth?

1:48 Whence knowest thou me?

1:50 Because I said unto thee, I saw thee under the fig tree, believest thou?

2:4 Woman, what have I to do with thee?

2:18 What sign shewest thou unto us, seeing that thou doest these things?

2:20 Forty and six years was this temple in building, and wilt thou rear it up in three days?

3:4 How can a man be born when he is old?

3:4 Can he enter the second time into his mother's womb, and be born?

3:9 How can these things be?

3:10 Art thou a master of Israel, and knowest not these things?

3:12 If I have told you earthly things, and ye believe not, how shall ye believe, if I tell you of heavenly things?

4:9 Then saith the woman of Samaria unto him, How is it that thou, being a Jew, askest drink of me, which am a woman of Samaria? for the Jews have no dealings with the Samaritans.

4:11 Sir, thou hast nothing to draw with, and the well is deep: from whence then hast thou that living water?

4:12 Art thou greater than our father Jacob, which gave us the well, and drank thereof himself, and his children, and his cattle?

4:27 What seekest thou?

4:27 Why talkest thou with her?

4:29 Come, see a man, which told me all things that ever I did: is not this the Christ?

4:33 Hath any man brought him ought to eat?

5:6 Wilt thou be made whole?

5:12 What man is that which said unto thee, Take up thy bed, and walk?

5:44 How can ye believe, which receive honour one of another, and seek not the honour that cometh from God only?

5:47 If ye believe not his writings, how shall ye believe my words?

6:5 Whence shall we buy bread, that these may eat?

6:9 There is a lad here, which hath five barley loaves, and two small fishes: but what are they among so many?

6:25 Rabbi, when camest thou hither?

6:28 What shall we do, that we might work the works of God?

6:30 What sign shewest thou then, that we may see, and believe thee?

6:30 What dost thou work?

6:42 Is not this Jesus, the son of Joseph, whose father and mother we know?

6:42 How is it then that he saith, I came down from heaven?

6:52 How can this man give us his flesh to eat?

6:60 This is an hard saying; who can hear it?

6:61 Doth this offend you?

6:62 What and if ye shall see the Son of man ascend up where he was before?

6:67 Will ye also go away?

6:68 Lord, to whom shall we go?

6:70 Have not I chosen you twelve, and one of you is a devil?

7:11 Where is he?

7:15 How knoweth this man letters, having never learned?

7:19 Did not Moses give you the law, and yet none of you keepeth the law?

7:19 Why go ye about to kill me?

7:20 Thou hast a devil: who goeth about to kill thee?

7:23 If a man on the sabbath day receive circumcision, that the law of Moses should not be broken; are ye angry at me, because I have made a man every whit whole on the sabbath day?

7:25 Is not this he, whom they seek to kill?

7:26 Do the rulers know indeed that this is the very Christ?

7:31 When Christ cometh, will he do more miracles than these which this man hath done?

7:35 Whither will he go, that we shall not find him?

7:35 Will he go unto the dispersed among the Gentiles, and teach the Gentiles?

7:36 What manner of saying is this that he said, Ye shall seek me, and shall not find me: and where I am, thither ye cannot come?

7:41 Shall Christ come out of Galilee?

7:42 Hath not the scripture said, That Christ cometh of the seed of David, and out of the town of Bethlehem, where David was?

7:45 Why have ye not brought him?

7:47 Are ye also deceived?

7:48 Have any of the rulers or of the Pharisees believed on him?

7:51 Doth our law judge any man, before it hear him, and know what he doeth?

7:52 Art thou also of Galilee?

8:5 Now Moses in the law commanded us, that such should be stoned: but what sayest thou?

8:10 Woman, where are those thine accusers?

8:10 Hath no man condemned thee?

8:19 Where is thy Father?

8:22 Will he kill himself?

8:25 Who art thou?

8:33 We be Abraham's seed, and were never in bondage to any man: how sayest thou, Ye shall be made free?

8:43 Why do ye not understand my speech?

8:46 Which of you convinceth me of sin?

8:46 And if I say the truth, why do ye not believe me?

8:48 Say we not well that thou art a Samaritan, and hast a devil?

8:53 Art thou greater than our father Abraham, which is dead?

8:53 Whom makest thou thyself?

8:57 Thou art not yet fifty years old, and hast thou seen Abraham?

9:2 Master, who did sin, this man, or his parents, that he was born blind?

9:8 Is not this he that sat and begged?

9:10 How were thine eyes opened?

9:12 Where is he?

9:16 How can a man that is a sinner do such miracles?

9:17 What sayest thou of him, that he hath opened thine eyes?

9:19 Is this your son, who ye say was born blind?

9:19 How then doth he now see?

9:26 What did he to thee?

9:26 How opened he thine eyes?

9:27 I have told you already, and ye did not hear: wherefore would ye hear it again?

9:27 Will ye also be his disciples?

9:34 Thou wast altogether born in sins, and dost thou teach us?

9:35 Dost thou believe on the Son of God?

9:36 Who is he, Lord, that I might believe on him?

9:40 Are we blind also?

10:20 He hath a devil, and is mad; why hear ye him?

10:21 Can a devil open the eyes of the blind?

10:24 How long dost thou make us to doubt?

10:32 Many good works have I shewed you from my Father; for which of those works do ye stone me?

10:34 Is it not written in your law, I said, Ye are gods?

10:36 Say ye of him, whom the Father hath sanctified, and sent into the world, Thou blasphemest; because I said, I am the Son of God?

11:8 Master, the Jews of late sought to stone thee; and goest thou thither again?

11:9 Are there not twelve hours in the day?

11:26 Whosoever liveth and believeth in me shall never die. Believest thou this?

11:34 Where have ye laid him?

11:37 Could not this man, which opened the eyes of the blind, have caused that even this man should not have died?

11:40 Said I not unto thee, that, if thou wouldest believe, thou shouldest see the glory of God?

11:47 What do we? for this man doeth many miracles.

11:56 What think ye, that he will not come to the feast?

12:5 Why was not this ointment sold for three hundred pence, and given to the poor?

12:19 Perceive ye how ye prevail nothing? behold, the world is gone after him.

12:27 Now is my soul troubled; and what shall I say?

12:34 We have heard out of the law that Christ abideth for ever: and how sayest thou, The Son of man must be lifted up?

12:34 Who is this Son of man?

12:38 Lord, who hath believed our report?

12:38 And to whom hath the arm of the Lord been revealed?

13:6 Lord, dost thou wash my feet?

13:12 Know ye what I have done to you?

13:25 Lord, who is it?

13:36 Lord, whither goest thou?

13:37 Lord, why cannot I follow thee now?

13:38 Wilt thou lay down thy life for my sake?

14:5 Lord, we know not whither thou goest; and how can we know the way?

14:9 Have I been so long time with you, and yet hast thou not known me, Philip?

14:9 He that hath seen me hath seen the Father; and how sayest thou then, Shew us the Father?

14:10 Believest thou not that I am in the Father, and the Father in me?

14:22 Lord, how is it that thou wilt manifest thyself unto us, and not unto the world?

16:5 But now I go my way to him that sent me; and none of you asketh me, Whither goest thou?

16:17 What is this that he saith unto us, A little while, and ye shall not see me: and again, a little while, and ye shall see me: and, Because I go to the Father?

16:18 What is this that he saith, A little while? we cannot tell what he saith.

16:19 Do ye enquire among yourselves of that I said, A little while, and ye shall not see me: and again, a little while, and ye shall see me?

16:31 Do ye now believe?

18:4 Whom seek ye?

18:7 Whom seek ye?

18:11 Put up thy sword into the sheath: the cup which my Father hath given me, shall I not drink it?

18:17 Art not thou also one of this man's disciples?

18:20 Why askest thou me?

18:22 Answerest thou the high priest so?

18:23 If I have spoken evil, bear witness of the evil: but if well, why smitest thou me?

18:25 Art not thou also one of his disciples?

18:26 Did not I see thee in the garden with him?

18:29 What accusation bring ye against this man?

18:29 Will ye therefore that I release unto you the King of the Jews?

18:33 Art thou the King of the Jews?

18:34 Sayest thou this thing of thyself, or did others tell it thee of me?

18:35 Am I a Jew?

18:35 Thine own nation and the chief priests have delivered thee unto me: what hast thou done?

18:37 Art thou a king then?

18:38 What is truth?

19:9 Whence art thou?

19:10 Speakest thou not unto me?

19:10 Knowest thou not that I have power to crucify thee, and have power to release thee?

19:15 Shall I crucify your King?

20:13 Woman, why weepest thou?

20:15 Woman, why weepest thou?

20:15 Whom seekest thou?

21:5 Children, have ye any meat?

21:12 Who art thou?

21:15 Simon, son of Jonas, lovest thou me more than these?

21:16 Simon, son of Jonas, lovest thou me?

21:17 Simon, son of Jonas, lovest thou me?

21:17 Lovest thou me?

21:20 Lord, which is he that betrayeth thee?

21:21 Lord, and what shall this man do?

21:22 If I will that he tarry till I come, what is that to thee? follow thou me.

21:23 Then went this saying abroad among the brethren, that that disciple should not die: yet Jesus said not unto him, He shall not die; but, If I will that he tarry till I come, what is that to thee?

CHURCH HISTORY

Sirs, ye are brethren; why do ye wrong one to another?
Acts 7:26

The Acts of the Apostles

1:6 Lord, wilt thou at this time restore again the kingdom to Israel?

1:11 Ye men of Galilee, why stand ye gazing up into heaven?

2:7 Behold, are not all these which speak Galilaeans?

2:8 And how hear we every man in our own tongue, wherein we were born?

2:12 What meaneth this?

2:37 Now when they heard this, they were pricked in their heart, and said unto Peter and to the rest of the apostles, Men and brethren, what shall we do?

3:12 Why marvel ye at this?

3:12 Or why look ye so earnestly on us, as though by our own power or holiness we had made this man to walk?

4:7 By what power, or by what name, have ye done this?

4:16 What shall we do to these men?

4:25 Why did the heathen rage, and the people imagine vain things?

5:3 Why hath Satan filled thine heart to lie to the Holy Ghost, and to keep back part of the price of the land?

5:4 Whiles it remained, was it not thine own?

5:4 And after it was sold, was it not in thine own power?

5:4 Why hast thou conceived this thing in thine heart?

5:8 Tell me whether ye sold the land for so much?

5:9 How is it that ye have agreed together to tempt the Spirit of the Lord?

5:28 Did not we straitly command you that ye should not teach in this name?

7:1 Are these things so?

7:26 Sirs, ye are brethren; why do ye wrong one to another?

7:27 Who made thee a ruler and a judge over us?

7:28 Wilt thou kill me, as thou diddest the Egyptian yesterday?

7:35 Who made thee a ruler and a judge?

7:42 O ye house of Israel, have ye offered to me slain beasts and sacrifices by the space of forty years in the wilderness?

7:49 Heaven is my throne, and earth is my footstool: what house will ye build me?

7:49 Saith the Lord: or what is the place of my rest?

7:50 Hath not my hand made all these things?

7:52 Which of the prophets have not your fathers persecuted?

8:30 Understandest thou what thou readest?

8:31 How can I, except some man should guide me?

8:33 In his humiliation his judgment was taken away: and who shall declare his generation? for his life is taken from the earth.

8:34 Of whom speaketh the prophet this?

8:34 Of himself, or of some other man?

8:36 What doth hinder me to be baptized?

9:4 Saul, Saul, why persecutest thou me?

9:5 Who art thou, Lord?

9:6 Lord, what wilt thou have me to do?

9:21 Is not this he that destroyed them which called on this name in Jerusalem, and came hither for that intent, that he might bring them bound unto the chief priests?

10:21 What is the cause wherefore ye are come?

10:29 For what intent ye have sent for me?

10:47 Can any man forbid water, that these should not be baptized, which have received the Holy Ghost as well as we?

11:17 What was I, that I could withstand God?

13:10 Wilt thou not cease to pervert the right ways of the Lord?

14:15 Why do ye these things?

15:10 Why tempt ye God, to put a yoke upon the neck of the disciples, which neither our fathers nor we were able to bear?

16:30 What must I do to be saved?

16:37 They have beaten us openly uncondemned, being Romans, and have cast us into prison; and now do they thrust us out privily?

17:18 What will this babbler say?

17:19 May we know what this new doctrine, whereof thou speakest, is?

19:2 Have ye received the Holy Ghost since ye believed?

19:3 Unto what then were ye baptized?

19:15 And the evil spirit answered and said, Jesus I know, and Paul I know; but who are ye?

19:35 What man is there that knoweth not how that the city of the Ephesians is a worshipper of the great goddess Diana, and of the image which fell down from Jupiter?

21:13 What mean ye to weep and to break mine heart?

21:22 What is it therefore?

21:37 May I speak unto thee?

21:37 Canst thou speak Greek?

21:38 Art not thou that Egyptian, which before these days madest an uproar, and leddest out into the wilderness four thousand men that were murderers?

22:7 Saul, Saul, why persecutest thou me?

22:8 Who art thou, Lord?

22:10 What shall I do, Lord?

22:16 Why tarriest thou?

22:25 Is it lawful for you to scourge a man that is a Roman, and uncondemned?

22:27 Tell me, art thou a Roman?

23:3 Sittest thou to judge me after the law, and commandest me to be smitten contrary to the law?

23:4 Revilest thou God's high priest?

23:19 What is that thou hast to tell me?

25:9 Wilt thou go up to Jerusalem, and there be judged of these things before me?

25:12 Hast thou appealed unto Caesar?

26:8 Why should it be thought a thing incredible with you, that God should raise the dead?

26:14 Saul, Saul, why persecutest thou me?

26:15 Who art thou, Lord?

26:27 Believest thou the prophets?

PAUL'S EPISTLES TO THE CHURCHES

Thinkest thou this, O man, that judgest them which do such things,
and doest the same, that thou shalt escape the judgment of God?
Romans 2:3

The Epistle of Paul the Apostle to the
Romans

2:3 Thinkest thou this, O man, that judgest them which do such things, and doest the same, that thou shalt escape the judgment of God?

2:4 Or despisest thou the riches of his goodness and forbearance and longsuffering; not knowing that the goodness of God leadeth thee to repentance?

2:21 Thou therefore which teachest another, teachest thou not thyself?

2:21 Thou that preachest a man should not steal, dost thou steal?

2:22 Thou that sayest a man should not commit adultery, dost thou commit adultery?

2:22 Thou that abhorrest idols, dost thou commit sacrilege?

2:23 Thou that makest thy boast of the law, through breaking the law dishonourest thou God?

2:26 If the uncircumcision keep the righteousness of the law, shall not his uncircumcision be counted for circumcision?

2:27 Shall not uncircumcision which is by nature, if it fulfil the law, judge thee, who by the letter and circumcision dost transgress the law?

3:1 What advantage then hath the Jew?

3:1 Or what profit is there of circumcision?

3:3 For what if some did not believe?

3:3 Shall their unbelief make the faith of God without effect?

3:5 But if our unrighteousness commend the righteousness of God, what shall we say?

3:5 Is God unrighteous who taketh vengeance? (I speak as a man.)

3:5 God forbid: for then how shall God judge the world?

3:7 For if the truth of God hath more abounded through my lie unto his glory; why yet am I also judged as a sinner?

3:9 And not rather, (as we be slanderously reported, and as some affirm that we say,) Let us do evil, that good may come? whose damnation is just.

3:9 What then?

3:9 Are we better than they?

3:27 Where is boasting then?

3:27 It is excluded. By what law?

3:27 Of works? Nay: but by the law of faith.

3:29 Is he the God of the Jews only?

3:29 Is he not also of the Gentiles?

3:31 Do we then make void the law through faith?

4:1 What shall we say then that Abraham our father, as pertaining to the flesh, hath found?

4:3 For what saith the scripture?

4:9 Cometh this blessedness then upon the circumcision only, or upon the uncircumcision also?

4:10 How was it then reckoned?

4:10 When he was in circumcision, or in uncircumcision?

6:1 What shall we say then?

6:1 Shall we continue in sin, that grace may abound?

6:2 How shall we, that are dead to sin, live any longer therein?

6:3 Know ye not, that so many of us as were baptized into Jesus Christ were baptized into his death?

6:15 What then?

6:15 Shall we sin, because we are not under the law, but under grace?

6:16 Know ye not, that to whom ye yield yourselves servants to obey, his servants ye are to whom ye obey; whether of sin unto death, or of obedience unto righteousness?

6:21 What fruit had ye then in those things whereof ye are now ashamed?

7:1 Know ye not, brethren, (for I speak to them that know the law,) how that the law hath dominion over a man as long as he liveth?

7:7 What shall we say then?

7:7 Is the law sin?

7:13 Was then that which is good made death unto me?

7:24 Who shall deliver me from the body of this death?

8:24 For we are saved by hope: but hope that is seen is not hope: for what a man seeth, why doth he yet hope for?

8:31 What shall we then say to these things?

8:31 If God be for us, who can be against us?

8:32 He that spared not his own Son, but delivered him up for us all, how shall he not with him also freely give us all things?

8:33 Who shall lay any thing to the charge of God's elect?

8:34 Who is he that condemneth?

8:35 Who shall separate us from the love of Christ?

8:35 Shall tribulation, or distress, or persecution, or famine, or nakedness, or peril, or sword?

9:14 What shall we say then?

9:14 Is there unrighteousness with God? God forbid.

9:19 Why doth he yet find fault?

9:19 For who hath resisted his will?

9:20 Who art thou that repliest against God?

9:20 Shall the thing formed say to him that formed it, Why hast thou made me thus?

9:21 Hath not the potter power over the clay, of the same lump to make one vessel unto honour, and another unto dishonour?

9:22, 23, 24 What if God, willing to shew his wrath, and to make his power known, endured with much longsuffering the vessels of wrath fitted to destruction: And that he might make known the riches of his glory on the vessels of mercy, which he had afore prepared unto glory, Even us, whom he hath called, not of the Jews only, but also of the Gentiles?

9:30 What shall we say then?

9:32 Wherefore?

10:6 Who shall ascend into heaven? (that is, to bring Christ down from above:)

10:7 Or, Who shall descend into the deep? (that is, to bring up Christ again from the dead.)

10:8 But what saith it?

10:14 How then shall they call on him in whom they have not believed?

10:14 And how shall they believe in him of whom they have not heard?

10:14 And how shall they hear without a preacher?

10:15 And how shall they preach, except they be sent?

10:16 For Esaias saith, Lord, who hath believed our report?

10:18 But I say, Have they not heard?

10:19 But I say, Did not Israel know?

11:1 I say then, Hath God cast away his people?

11:2 Wot ye not what the scripture saith of Elias?

11:4 But what saith the answer of God unto him?

11:7 What then?

11:11 I say then, Have they stumbled that they should fall?

11:12 Now if the fall of them be the riches of the world, and the diminishing of them the riches of the Gentiles; how much more their fulness?

11:15 For if the casting away of them be the reconciling of the world, what shall the receiving of them be, but life from the dead?

11:24 For if thou wert cut out of the olive tree which is wild by nature, and wert graffed contrary to nature into a good olive tree: how much more shall these, which be the natural branches, be graffed into their own olive tree?

11:34 For who hath known the mind of the Lord?

11:34 Or who hath been his counsellor?

11:35 Or who hath first given to him, and it shall be recompensed unto him again?

13:3 Wilt thou then not be afraid of the power?

14:4 Who art thou that judgest another man's servant?

14:10 But why dost thou judge thy brother?

14:10 Or why dost thou set at nought thy brother?

14:22 Hast thou faith?

The First Epistle of Paul the Apostle to the
Corinthians

1:13 Is Christ divided?

1:13 Was Paul crucified for you?

1:13 Or were ye baptized in the name of Paul?

1:20 Where is the wise?

1:20 Where is the scribe?

1:20 Where is the disputer of this world?

1:20 Hath not God made foolish the wisdom of this world?

2:11 For what man knoweth the things of a man, save the spirit of man which is in him?

2:16 For who hath known the mind of the Lord, that he may instruct him?

3:3 For whereas there is among you envying, and strife, and divisions, are ye not carnal, and walk as men?

3:4 For while one saith, I am of Paul; and another, I am of Apollos; are ye not carnal?

3:5 Who then is Paul, and who is Apollos, but ministers by whom ye believed, even as the Lord gave to every man?

3:16 Know ye not that ye are the temple of God, and that the Spirit of God dwelleth in you?

4:7 For who maketh thee to differ from another?

4:7 And what hast thou that thou didst not receive?

4:7 Now if thou didst receive it, why dost thou glory, as if thou hadst not received it?

4:21 What will ye?

4:21 Shall I come unto you with a rod, or in love, and in the spirit of meekness?

5:6 Know ye not that a little leaven leaveneth the whole lump?

5:12 For what have I to do to judge them also that are without?

5:12 Do not ye judge them that are within?

6:1 Dare any of you, having a matter against another, go to law before the unjust, and not before the saints?

6:2 Do ye not know that the saints shall judge the world?

6:2 And if the world shall be judged by you, are ye unworthy to judge the smallest matters?

6:3 Know ye not that we shall judge angels?

6:3 How much more things that pertain to this life?

6:5 Is it so, that there is not a wise man among you?

6:5 No, not one that shall be able to judge between his brethren?

6:7 Why do ye not rather take wrong?

6:7 Why do ye not rather suffer yourselves to be defrauded?

6:9 Know ye not that the unrighteous shall not inherit the kingdom of God?

6:15 Know ye not that your bodies are the members of Christ?

6:15 Shall I then take the members of Christ, and make them the members of an harlot?

6:16 What?

6:16 Know ye not that he which is joined to an harlot is one body?

6:19 What?

6:19 Know ye not that your body is the temple of the Holy Ghost which is in you, which ye have of God, and ye are not your own?

7:16 For what knowest thou, O wife, whether thou shalt save thy husband?

7:16 Or how knowest thou, O man, whether thou shalt save thy wife?

7:18 Is any man called being circumcised?

7:18 Is any called in uncircumcision?

7:21 Art thou called being a servant?

7:27 Art thou bound unto a wife?

7:27 Art thou loosed from a wife?

8:10, 11 For if any man see thee which hast knowledge sit at meat in the idol's temple, shall not the conscience of him which is weak be emboldened to eat those things which are offered to idols; And through thy knowledge shall the weak brother perish, for whom Christ died?

9:1 Am I not an apostle?

9:1 Am I not free?

9:1 Have I not seen Jesus Christ our Lord?

9:1 Are not ye my work in the Lord?

9:4 Have we not power to eat and to drink?

9:5 Have we not power to lead about a sister, a wife, as well as other apostles, and as the brethren of the Lord, and Cephas?

9:6 Or I only and Barnabas, have not we power to forbear working?

9:7 Who goeth a warfare any time at his own charges?

9:7 Who planteth a vineyard, and eateth not of the fruit thereof?

9:7 Or who feedeth a flock, and eateth not of the milk of the flock?

9:8 Say I these things as a man?

9:8 Or saith not the law the same also?

9:10 Doth God take care for oxen?

9:10 Or saith he it altogether for our sakes?

9:11 If we have sown unto you spiritual things, is it a great thing if we shall reap your carnal things?

9:12 If others be partakers of this power over you, are not we rather?

9:13 Do ye not know that they which minister about holy things live of the things of the temple?

9:13 And they which wait at the altar are partakers with the altar?

9:18 What is my reward then?

9:24 Know ye not that they which run in a race run all, but one receiveth the prize?

10:16 The cup of blessing which we bless, is it not the communion of the blood of Christ?

10:16 The bread which we break, is it not the communion of the body of Christ?

10:18 Are not they which eat of the sacrifices partakers of the altar?

10:19 What say I then?

10:19 That the idol is any thing, or that which is offered in sacrifice to idols is any thing?

10:22 Do we provoke the Lord to jealousy?

10:22 Are we stronger than he?

10:29 For why is my liberty judged of another man's conscience?

10:30 Why am I evil spoken of for that for which I give thanks?

11:13 Is it comely that a woman pray unto God uncovered?

11:14 Doth not even nature itself teach you, that, if a man have long hair, it is a shame unto him?

11:22 What?

11:22 Have ye not houses to eat and to drink in?

11:22 Or despise ye the church of God, and shame them that have not?

11:22 What shall I say to you?

11:22 Shall I praise you in this?

12:15 If the foot shall say, Because I am not the hand, I am not of the body; is it therefore not of the body?

12:16 And if the ear shall say, Because I am not the eye, I am not of the body; is it therefore not of the body?

12:17 If the whole body were an eye, where were the hearing?

12:17 If the whole were hearing, where were the smelling?

12:19 And if they were all one member, where were the body?

12:29 Are all apostles?

12:29 Are all prophets?

12:29 Are all teachers?

12:29 Are all workers of miracles?

12:30 Have all the gifts of healing?

12:30 Do all speak with tongues?

12:30 Do all interpret?

14:6 If I come unto you speaking with tongues, what shall I profit you, except I shall speak to you either by revelation, or by knowledge, or by prophesying, or by doctrine?

14:7 And even things without life giving sound, whether pipe or harp, except they give a distinction in the sounds, how shall it be known what is piped or harped?

14:8 For if the trumpet give an uncertain sound, who shall prepare himself to the battle?

14:15 What is it then?

14:16 Else when thou shalt bless with the spirit, how shall he that occupieth the room of the unlearned say Amen at thy giving of thanks, seeing he understandeth not what thou sayest?

14:23 If therefore the whole church be come together into one place, and all speak with tongues, and there come in those that are unlearned, or unbelievers, will they not say that ye are mad?

14:26 How is it then, brethren? when ye come together, every one of you hath a psalm, hath a doctrine, hath a tongue, hath a revelation, hath an interpretation. Let all things be done unto edifying.

14:36 What?

14:36 Came the word of God out from you?

14:36 Or came it unto you only?

15:12 Now if Christ be preached that he rose from the dead, how say some among you that there is no resurrection of the dead?

15:29 Else what shall they do which are baptized for the dead, if the dead rise not at all?

15:29 Why are they then baptized for the dead?

15:30 And why stand we in jeopardy every hour?

15:35 How are the dead raised up?

15:35 And with what body do they come?

15:55 O death, where is thy sting?

15:55 O grave, where is thy victory?

The Second Epistle of Paul the Apostle to the
Corinthians

1:17 When I therefore was thus minded, did I use lightness?

1:17 Or the things that I purpose, do I purpose according to the flesh, that with me there should be yea yea, and nay nay?

2:2 For if I make you sorry, who is he then that maketh me glad, but the same which is made sorry by me?

2:16 To the one we are the savour of death unto death; and to the other the savour of life unto life. And who is sufficient for these things?

3:1 Do we begin again to commend ourselves?

3:1 Or need we, as some others, epistles of commendation to you, or letters of commendation from you?

3:8 How shall not the ministration of the spirit be rather glorious?

6:14 For what fellowship hath righteousness with unrighteousness?

6:14 And what communion hath light with darkness?

6:15 And what concord hath Christ with Belial?

6:15 Or what part hath he that believeth with an infidel?

6:16 And what agreement hath the temple of God with idols?

10:7 Do ye look on things after the outward appearance?

11:7 Have I committed an offence in abasing myself that ye might be exalted, because I have preached to you the gospel of God freely?

11:11 Wherefore?

11:11 Because I love you not?

11:22 Are they Hebrews? so am I.

11:22 Are they Israelites? so am I.

11:22 Are they the seed of Abraham? so am I.

11:23 Are they ministers of Christ?

11:29 Who is weak, and I am not weak?

11:29 Who is offended, and I burn not?

12:13 For what is it wherein ye were inferior to other churches, except it be that I myself was not burdensome to you? forgive me this wrong.

12:17 Did I make a gain of you by any of them whom I sent unto you?

12:18 Did Titus make a gain of you?

12:18 Walked we not in the same spirit?

12:18 Walked we not in the same steps?

12:19 Again, think ye that we excuse ourselves unto you?

13:5 Know ye not your own selves, how that Jesus Christ is in you, except ye be reprobates?

The Epistle of Paul the Apostle to the
Galatians

1:10 For do I now persuade men, or God?

1:10 Or do I seek to please men?

2:14 I said unto Peter before them all, If thou, being a Jew, livest after the manner of Gentiles, and not as do the Jews, why compellest thou the Gentiles to live as do the Jews?

2:17 But if, while we seek to be justified by Christ, we ourselves also are found sinners, is therefore Christ the minister of sin? God forbid.

3:1 O foolish Galatians, who hath bewitched you, that ye should not obey the truth, before whose eyes Jesus Christ hath been evidently set forth, crucified among you?

3:2 This only would I learn of you, Received ye the Spirit by the works of the law, or by the hearing of faith?

3:3 Are ye so foolish?

3:3 Having begun in the Spirit, are ye now made perfect by the flesh?

3:4 Have ye suffered so many things in vain?

3:5 He therefore that ministereth to you the Spirit, and worketh miracles among you, doeth he it by the works of the law, or by the hearing of faith?

3:19 Wherefore then serveth the law?

3:21 Is the law then against the promises of God?

4:9 But now, after that ye have known God, or rather are known of God, how turn ye again to the weak and beggarly elements, whereunto ye desire again to be in bondage?

4:15 Where is then the blessedness ye spake of?

4:16 Am I therefore become your enemy, because I tell you the truth?

4:21 Tell me, ye that desire to be under the law, do ye not hear the law?

4:30 Nevertheless what saith the scripture?

5:7 Ye did run well; who did hinder you that ye should not obey the truth?

5:11 And I, brethren, if I yet preach circumcision, why do I yet suffer persecution? then is the offence of the cross ceased.

The Epistle of Paul the Apostle to the
Ephesians

4:9, 10 (Now that he ascended, what is it but that he also descended first into the lower parts of the earth? He that descended is the same also that ascended up far above all heavens, that he might fill all things.)

The Epistle of Paul the Apostle to the
Philippians

1:18 What then? notwithstanding, every way, whether in pretence, or in truth, Christ is preached; and I therein do rejoice, yea, and will rejoice.

The Epistle of Paul the Apostle to the
Colossians

2:20, 21, 22 Wherefore if ye be dead with Christ from the rudiments of the world, why, as though living in the world, are ye subject to ordinances, (Touch not; taste not; handle not; Which all are to perish with the using;) after the commandments and doctrines of men?

The First Epistle of Paul the Apostle to the
Thessalonians

2:19 For what is our hope, or joy, or crown of rejoicing?

2:19 Are not even ye in the presence of our Lord Jesus Christ at his coming?

3:9, 10 For what thanks can we render to God again for you, for all the joy wherewith we joy for your sakes before our God; Night and day praying exceedingly that we might see your face, and might perfect that which is lacking in your faith?

The Second Epistle of Paul the Apostle to the
Thessalonians

2:5 Remember ye not, that, when I was yet with you, I told you these things?

PAUL'S EPISTLES
TO FRIENDS

*(For if a man know not how to rule his own house,
how shall he take care of the church of God?)*
1 Timothy 3:5

The First Epistle of Paul the Apostle to
Timothy

3:5 (For if a man know not how to rule his own house, how shall he take care of the church of God?)

The Second Epistle of Paul the Apostle to
Timothy

No questions are found in 2 Timothy.

The Epistle of Paul to
Titus

No questions are found in the book of Titus.

The Epistle of Paul to
Philemon

1:16 For perhaps he therefore departed for a season, that thou shouldest receive him for ever; Not now as a servant, but above a servant, a brother beloved, specially to me, but how much more unto thee, both in the flesh, and in the Lord?

GENERAL EPISTLES

GENERAL EPISTLES

Furthermore we have had fathers of our flesh which corrected us, and we gave them reverence: shall we not much rather be in subjection unto the Father of spirits, and live?
Hebrews 12:9

The Epistle of Paul the Apostle to the
Hebrews

1:5 For unto which of the angels said he at any time, Thou art my Son, this day have I begotten thee?

1:5 And again, I will be to him a Father, and he shall be to me a Son?

1:14 Are they not all ministering spirits, sent forth to minister for them who shall be heirs of salvation?

2:3, 4 How shall we escape, if we neglect so great salvation; which at the first began to be spoken by the Lord, and was confirmed unto us by them that heard him; God also bearing them witness, both with signs and wonders, and with divers miracles, and gifts of the Holy Ghost, according to his own will?

2:6 What is man, that thou art mindful of him?

2:6 Or the son of man, that thou visitest him?

3:17 Was it not with them that had sinned, whose carcases fell in the wilderness?

3:18 And to whom sware he that they should not enter into his rest, but to them that believed not?

3:16, 17 For some, when they had heard, did provoke: howbeit not all that came out of Egypt by Moses. But with whom was he grieved forty years?

7:11 If therefore perfection were by the Levitical priesthood, (for under it the people received the law,) what further need was there that another priest should rise after the order of Melchisedec, and not be called after the order of Aaron?

9:14 For if the blood of bulls and of goats, and the ashes of an heifer sprinkling the unclean, sanctifieth to the purifying of the flesh: How much more shall the blood of Christ, who through the eternal Spirit offered himself without spot to God, purge your conscience from dead works to serve the living God?

10:1, 2 For the law having a shadow of good things to come, and not the very image of the things, can never with those sacrifices which they offered year by year continually make the comers thereunto perfect. For then would they not have ceased to be offered? because that the worshippers once purged should have had no more conscience of sins.

10:28, 29 He that despised Moses' law died without mercy under two or three witnesses: Of how much sorer punishment, suppose ye, shall he be thought worthy, who hath trodden under foot the Son of God, and hath counted the blood of the covenant, wherewith he was sanctified, an unholy thing, and hath done despite unto the Spirit of grace?

11:32 What shall I more say?

12:7 If ye endure chastening, God dealeth with you as with sons; for what son is he whom the father chasteneth not?

12:9 Furthermore we have had fathers of our flesh which corrected us, and we gave them reverence: shall we not much rather be in subjection unto the Father of spirits, and live?

The General Epistle of
James

2:2, 3, 4 For if there come unto your assembly a man with a gold ring, in goodly apparel, and there come in also a poor man in vile raiment; And ye have respect to him that weareth the gay clothing, and say unto him, Sit thou here in a good place; and say to the poor, Stand thou there, or sit here under my footstool: Are ye not then partial in yourselves, and are become judges of evil thoughts?

2:5 Hearken, my beloved brethren, Hath not God chosen the poor of this world rich in faith, and heirs of the kingdom which he hath promised to them that love him?

2:6 But ye have despised the poor. Do not rich men oppress you, and draw you before the judgment seats?

2:7 Do not they blaspheme that worthy name by the which ye are called?

2:14 What doth it profit, my brethren, though a man say he hath faith, and have not works?

2:14 Can faith save him?

2:20 But wilt thou know, O vain man, that faith without works is dead?

2:21 Was not Abraham our father justified by works, when he had offered Isaac his son upon the altar?

2:22 Seest thou how faith wrought with his works, and by works was faith made perfect?

2:25 Likewise also was not Rahab the harlot justified by works, when she had received the messengers, and had sent them out another way?

2:15, 16 If a brother or sister be naked, and destitute of daily food, And one of you say unto them, Depart in peace, be ye warmed and filled;

notwithstanding ye give them not those things which are needful to the body; what doth it profit?

3:11 Doth a fountain send forth at the same place sweet water and bitter?

3:12 Can the fig tree, my brethren, bear olive berries?

3:12 Either a vine, figs? so can no fountain both yield salt water and fresh.

3:13 Who is a wise man and endued with knowledge among you? let him shew out of a good conversation his works with meekness of wisdom.

4:1 From whence come wars and fightings among you?

4:1 Come they not hence, even of your lusts that war in your members?

4:4 Ye adulterers and adulteresses, know ye not that the friendship of the world is enmity with God? whosoever therefore will be a friend of the world is the enemy of God.

4:5 Do ye think that the scripture saith in vain, The spirit that dwelleth in us lusteth to envy?

4:12 There is one lawgiver, who is able to save and to destroy: who art thou that judgest another?

4:14 Whereas ye know not what shall be on the morrow. For wha tis your life? It is even a vapour, that appeareth for a little time, and then vanisheth away.

5:13 Is any among you afflicted?

5:13 Is any merry?

5:14 Is any sick among you?

The First Epistle General of
Peter

3:13 And who is he that will harm you, if ye be followers of that which is good?

4:17 For the time is come that judgment must begin at the house of God: and if it first begin at us, what shall the end be of them that obey not the gospel of God?

4:18 And if the righteous scarcely be saved, where shall the ungodly and the sinner appear?

The Second Epistle General of
Peter

3:3, 4 Knowing this first, that there shall come in the last days scoffers, walking after their own lusts, And saying, Where is the promise of his coming?

3:11, 12 What manner of persons ought ye to be in all holy conversation and godliness, Looking for and hasting unto the coming of the day of God, wherein the heavens being on fire shall be dissolved, and the elements shall melt with fervent heat?

The First Epistle General of
John

3:12 For this is the message that ye heard from the beginning, that we should love one another. Not as Cain, who was of that wicked one, and slew his brother. And wherefore slew he him? Because his own works were evil, and his brother's righteous.

3:17 But whoso hath this world's good, and seeth his brother have need, and shutteth up his bowels of compassion from him, how dwelleth the love of God in him?

4:20 If a man say, I love God, and hateth his brother, he is a liar: for he that loveth not his brother whom he hath seen, how can he love God whom he hath not seen?

5:5 Who is he that overcometh the world, but he that believeth that Jesus is the Son of God?

The Second Epistle of
John

No questions are found in 2 John.

The Third Epistle of
John

No questions are found in 3 John.

The General Epistle of
Jude

No questions are found in the book of Jude.

APOCALYPTIC

And one of the elders answered, saying unto me, What
are these which are arrayed in white robes?
Revelation 7:13

The
Revelation of Jesus

5:1, 2 And I saw in the right hand of him that sat on the throne a book written within and on the backside, sealed with seven seals. And I saw a strong angel proclaiming with a loud voice, Who is worthy to open the book, and to loose the seals thereof?

6:9, 10 And when he had opened the fifth seal, I saw under the altar the souls of them that were slain for the word of God, and for the testimony which they held: And they cried with a loud voice, saying, How long, O Lord, holy and true, dost thou not judge and avenge our blood on them that dwell on the earth?

6:17 For the great day of his wrath is come; and who shall be able to stand?

7:13 And one of the elders answered, saying unto me, What are these which are arrayed in white robes?

7:13 And whence came they?

13:4 And they worshipped the dragon which gave power unto the beast: and they worshipped the beast, saying, Who is like unto the beast?

13:4 Who is able to make war with him?

17:7 And the angel said unto me, Wherefore didst thou marvel? I will tell thee the mystery of the woman, and of the beast that carrieth her, which hath the seven heads and ten horns.

CATEGORIZED
GOSPEL QUESTIONS

What think ye of Christ?
Matthew 22:42

Questions Jesus Asked

The Gospel According to
Matthew

5:13 If the salt have lost his savour, wherewith shall it be salted?

5:46 If ye love them which love you, what reward have ye?

5:46 Do not even the publicans the same?

5:47 If ye salute your brethren only, what do ye more than others?

5:47 Do not even the publicans so?

6:25 Is not the life more than meat, and the body than raiment?

6:26 Are ye not much better than they?

6:27 Which of you by taking thought can add one cubit unto his stature?

6:28 Why take ye thought for raiment?

6:30 If God so clothe the grass of the field, which to day is, and to morrow is cast into the oven, shall he not much more clothe you, O ye of little faith?

6:31 What shall we eat?

6:31 What shall we drink?

6:31 Wherewithal shall we be clothed?

7:3 Why beholdest thou the mote that is in thy brother's eye, but considerest not the beam that is in thine own eye?

7:4 How wilt thou say to thy brother, Let me pull out the mote out of thine eye; and, behold, a beam is in thine own eye?

7:9 What man is there of you, whom if his son ask bread, will he give him a stone?

7:10 Or if he ask a fish, will he give him a serpent?

7:11 If ye then, being evil, know how to give good gifts unto your children, how much more shall your Father which is in heaven give good things to them that ask him?

7:16 Do men gather grapes of thorns, or figs of thistles?

7:22 Lord, Lord, have we not prophesied in thy name?

7:22 And in thy name have cast out devils?

7:22 And in thy name done many wonderful works?

8:26 Why are ye fearful, O ye of little faith?

9:4 Wherefore think ye evil in your hearts?

9:5 Whether is easier, to say, Thy sins be forgiven thee; or to say, Arise, and walk?

9:15 Can the children of the bridechamber mourn, as long as the bridegroom is with them?

9:28 Believe ye that I am able to do this?

10:25 If they have called the master of the house Beelzebub, how much more shall they call them of his household?

10:29 Are not two sparrows sold for a farthing?

11:7 What went ye out into the wilderness to see?

11:7 A reed shaken with the wind?

11:8 But what went ye out for to see?

11:8 A man clothed in soft raiment?

11:9 But what went ye out for to see?

11:9 A prophet?

11:16 Whereunto shall I liken this generation?

12:3, 4 Have ye not read what david did, when he was an hungered, and they that were with him; How he entered into the house of God, and did eat the shewbread, which was not lawful for him to eat, neither for them which were with him, but only the priests?

12:5 Or have ye not read in the law, how that on the sabbath days the priests in the temple profane the sabbath, and are blameless?

12:11 What man shall there be among you, that shall have one sheep, and if it fall into a pit on the sabbath day, will he not lay hold on it, and lift it out?

12:12 How much then is a man better than a sheep?

12:26 If Satan cast out Satan, he is divided against himself; how shall then his kingdom stand?

12:27 And if I by Beelzebub cast out devils, by whom do your children cast them out?

12:29 how can one enter into a strong man's house, and spoil his goods, except he first bind the strong man? and then he will spoil his house.

12:34 How can ye, being evil, speak good things?

12:48 Who is my mother?

12:48 Who are my brethren?

13:51 Have ye understood all these things?

14:31 Wherefore didst thou doubt?

15:3 Why do ye also transgress the commandment of God by your tradition?

15:16 Are ye also yet without understanding?

15:17 Do not ye yet understand, that whatsoever entereth in at the mouth goeth into the belly, and is cast out into the draught?

15:34 How many loaves have ye?

16:3 Can ye not discern the signs of the times?

16:8 Why reason ye among yourselves, because ye have brought no bread?

16:9 Do ye not yet understand, neither remember the five loaves of the five thousand, and how many baskets ye took up?

16:10 Neither the seven loaves of the four thousand, and how many baskets ye took up?

16:11 How is it that ye do not understand that I spake it not to you concerning bread, that ye should beware of the leaven of the Pharisees and of the Sadducees?

16:13 Whom do men say that I the Son of man am?

16:15 But whom say ye that I am?

16:26 For what is a man profited, if he shall gain the whole world, and lose his own soul?

16:26 or what shall a man give in exchange for his soul?

17:17 How long shall I be with you?

17:17 How long shall I suffer you?

17:25 What thinkest thou, Simon?

17:25 Of whom do the kings of the earth take custom or tribute?

17:25 Of their own children, or of strangers?

18:12 How think ye?

18:12 If a man have an hundred sheep, and one of them be gone astray, doth he not leave the ninety and nine, and goeth into the mountains, and seeketh that which is gone astray?

18:33 Shouldest not thou also have had compassion on thy fellowservant, even as I had pity on thee?

19:4, 5 Have ye not read, that he which made them at the beginning made them male and female, And said, For this cause shall a man leave father and mother, and shall cleave to his wife: and they twain shall be one flesh?

19:17 Why callest thou me good?

20:6 Why stand ye here all the day idle?

20:13 I do thee no wrong: didst not thou agree with me for a penny?

20:15 Is it not lawful for me to do what I will with mine own?

20:15 Is thine eye evil, because I am good?

20:21 What wilt thou?

20:22 Are ye able to drink of the cup that I shall drink of, and to be baptized with the baptism that I am baptized with?

20:32 What will ye that I shall do unto you?

21:16 Have ye never read, Out of the mouth of babes and sucklings thou hast perfected praise?

21:25 The baptism of John, whence was it?

21:25 From heaven, or of men?

21:28 What think ye?

21:31 Whether of them twain did the will of his father?

21:40 When the lord therefore of the vineyard cometh, what will he do unto those husbandmen?

21:42 Did ye never read in the scriptures, The stone which the builders rejected, the same is become the head of the corner: this is the Lord's doing, and it is marvellous in our eyes?

22:12 Friend, how camest thou in hither not having a wedding garment?

22:18 Why tempt ye me, ye hypocrites?

22:20 Whose is this image and superscription?

22:32 Have ye not read that which was spoken unto you by God, saying, I am the God of Abraham, and the God of Isaac, and the God of Jacob? God is not the God of the dead, but of the living.

22:42 What think ye of Christ?

22:42 Whose son is he?

22:43, 44 How then doth David in spirit call him Lord, saying, The LORD said unto my Lord, Sit thou on my right hand, till I make thine enemies thy footstool?

22:45 If David then call him Lord, how is he his son?

23:17 Whether is greater, the gold, or the temple that sanctifieth the gold?

23:19 Whether is greater, the gift, or the altar that sanctifieth the gift?

23:33 How can ye escape the damnation of hell?

24:2 See ye not all these things?

24:25 Who then is a faithful and wise servant, whom his lord hath made ruler over his household, to give them meat in due season?

26:10 Why trouble ye the woman?

26:40 What, could ye not watch with me one hour?

26:50 Friend, wherefore art thou come?

26:53 Thinkest thou that I cannot now pray to my Father, and he shall presently give me more than twelve legions of angels?

26:54 But how then shall the scriptures be fulfilled, that thus it must be?

26:55 Are ye come out as against a thief with swords and staves for to take me?

27:46 Eli, Eli, lama sabachthani?

27:46 My God, my God, why hast thou forsaken me?

The Gospel according to
Mark

2:8 Why reason ye these things in your hearts?

2:9 Whether is it easier to say to the sick of the palsy, Thy sins be forgiven thee; or to say, Arise, and take up thy bed, and walk?

2:19 Can the children of the bridechamber fast, while the bridegroom is with them?

2:25 Have ye never read what David did, when he had need, and was an hungred, he, and they that were with him?

2:26 How he went into the house of God in the days of Abiathar the high priest, and did eat the shewbread, which is not lawful to eat but for the priests, and gave also to them which were with him?

3:4 Is it lawful to do good on the sabbath days, or to do evil?

3:4 To save life, or to kill?

3:23 How can Satan cast out Satan?

3:33 Who is my mother, or my brethren?

4:13 Know ye not this parable?

4:13 And how then will ye know all parables?

4:21 Is a candle brought to be put under a bushel, or under a bed?

4:21 And not to be set on a candlestick?

4:30 Whereunto shall we liken the kingdom of God?

4:30 Or with what comparison shall we compare it?

4:40 Why are ye so fearful?

4:40 How is it that ye have no faith?

5:9 What is thy name?

5:30 Who touched my clothes?

5:31 Who touched me?

5:39 Why make ye this ado, and weep?

6:38 How many loaves have ye?

7:18 Are ye so without understanding also?

7:18,19 Do ye not perceive, that whatsoever thing from without entereth into the man, it cannot defile him; Because it entereth not into his heart, but into the belly, and goeth out into the draught, purging all meats?

8:4 From whence can a man satisfy these men with bread here in the wilderness?

8:5 How many loaves have ye?

8:12 Why doth this generation seek after a sign?

8:17 Why reason ye, because ye have no bread?

8:17 Perceive ye not yet, neither understand?

8:17 Have ye your heart yet hardened?

8:18 Having eyes, see ye not?

8:18 And having ears, hear ye not?

8:18 And do ye not remember?

8:19 When I brake the five loaves among five thousand, how many baskets full of fragments took ye up?

8:20 And when the seven among four thousand, how many baskets full of fragments took ye up?

8:21 How is it that ye do not understand?

8:27 Whom do men say that I am?

8:29 But whom say ye that I am?

8:37 For what shall it profit a man, if he shall gain the whole world, and lose his own soul?

8:37 Or what shall a man give in exchange for his soul?

9:16 What question ye with them?

9:19 O faithless generation, how long shall I be with you?

9:19 How long shall I suffer you?

9:21 How long is it ago since this came unto him?

9:33 What was it that ye disputed among yourselves by the way?

9:50 Salt is good: but if the salt have lost his saltness, wherewith will ye season it?

10:3 What did Moses command you?

10:18 Why callest thou me good?

10:36 What would ye that I should do for you?

10:38 Ye know not what ye ask: can ye drink of the cup that I drink of?

10:38 And be baptized with the baptism that I am baptized with?

10:51 What wilt thou that I should do unto thee?

11:3 Why do ye this?

11:17 Is it not written, My house shall be called of all nations the house of prayer?

11:30 The baptism of John, was it from heaven, or of men?

12:9 What shall therefore the lord of the vineyard do?

12:11 Have ye not read this scripture; The stone which the builders rejected is become the head of the corner: This was the Lord's doing, and it is marvellous in our eyes?

12:15 Why tempt ye me?

12:16 Whose is this image and superscription?

12:24 Do ye not therefore err, because ye know not the scriptures, neither the power of God?

12:26 Have ye not read in the book of Moses, how in the bush God spake unto him, saying, I am the God of Abraham, and the God of Isaac, and the God of Jacob?

12:35 How say the scribes that Christ is the Son of David?

12:37 David therefore himself calleth him Lord; and whence is he then his son?

13:2 Seest thou these great buildings?

14:6 Let her alone; why trouble ye her?

14:14 The Master saith, Where is the guest chamber, where I shall eat the passover with my disciples?

14:37 He cometh, and findeth them sleeping, and saith unto Peter, Simon, sleepest thou?

14:37 Couldest not thou watch one hour?

14:48 Are ye come out, as against a thief, with swords and with staves to take me?

15:34 Eloi, Eloi, lama sabachthani?

15:34 My God, my God, why hast thou forsaken me?

The Gospel according to
Luke

2:49 How is it that ye sought me?

2:49 Wist ye not that I must be about my Father's business?

5:22 What reason ye in your hearts?

5:23 Whether is easier, to say, Thy sins be forgiven thee; or to say, Rise up and walk?

5:34 Can ye make the children of the bridechamber fast, while the bridegroom is with them?

6:3,4 Have ye not read so much as this, what David did, when himself was an hungred, and they which were with him; How he went into the house of God, and did take and eat the shewbread, and gave also to them that were with him; which it is not lawful to eat but for the priests alone?

6:9 Is it lawful on the sabbath days to do good, or to do evil?

6:9 To save life, or to destroy it?

6:32 For if ye love them which love you, what thank have ye?

6:33 And if ye do good to them which do good to you, what thank have ye?

6:34 And if ye lend to them of whom ye hope to receive, what thank have ye?

6:39 Can the blind lead the blind?

6:39 Shall they not both fall into the ditch?

6:41 Why beholdest thou the mote that is in thy brother's eye, but perceivest not the beam that is in thine own eye?

6:42 How canst thou say to thy brother, Brother, let me pull out the mote that is in thine eye, when thou thyself beholdest not the beam that is in thine own eye?

6:46 Why call ye me, Lord, Lord, and do not the things which I say?

7:24 What went ye out into the wilderness for to see?

7:24 A reed shaken with the wind?

7:25 But what went ye out for to see?

7:25 A man clothed in soft raiment?

7:26 But what went ye out for to see?

7:26 A prophet?

7:31 Whereunto then shall I liken the men of this generation?

7:31 And to what are they like?

7:42 Which of them will love him most?

7:44 Seest thou this woman?

8:25 Where is your faith?

8:30 What is thy name?

8:45 Who touched me?

9:18 Whom say the people that I am?

9:20 But whom say ye that I am?

9:25 For what is a man advantaged, if he gain the whole world, and lose himself, or be cast away?

9:41 How long shall I be with you, and suffer you?

10:26 What is written in the law?

10:26 How readest thou?

10:36 Which now of these three, thinkest thou, was neighbour unto him that fell among the thieves?

11:6 Which of you shall have a friend, and shall go unto him at midnight, and say unto him, Friend, lend me three loaves; For a friend of mine in his journey is come to me, and I have nothing to set before him?

11:11 If a son shall ask bread of any of you that is a father, will he give him a stone?

11:11 Or if he ask a fish, will he for a fish give him a serpent?

11:12 Or if he shall ask an egg, will he offer him a scorpion?

11:13 If ye then, being evil, know how to give good gifts unto your children: how much more shall your heavenly Father give the Holy Spirit to them that ask him?

11:18 If Satan also be divided against himself, how shall his kingdom stand?

11:19 And if I by Beelzebub cast out devils, by whom do your sons cast them out?

11:40 Did not he that made that which is without make that which is within also?

12:6 Are not five sparrows sold for two farthings, and not one of them is forgotten before God?

12:14 Man, who made me a judge or a divider over you?

12:17 What shall I do, because I have no room where to bestow my fruits?

12:20 Whose shall those things be, which thou hast provided?

12:24 How much more are ye better than the fowls?

12:25 Which of you with taking thought can add to his stature one cubit?

12:26 If ye then be not able to do that thing which is least, why take ye thought for the rest?

12:28 If then God so clothe the grass, which is to day in the field, and to morrow is cast into the oven; how much more will he clothe you, O ye of little faith?

12:42 Who then is that faithful and wise steward, whom his lord shall make ruler over his household, to give them their portion of meat in due season?

12:49 I am come to send fire on the earth; and what will I, if it be already kindled?

12:51 Suppose ye that I am come to give peace on earth?

12:56 How is it that ye do not discern this time?

12:57 Yea, and why even of yourselves judge ye not what is right?

13:2 Suppose ye that these Galilaeans were sinners above all the Galilaeans, because they suffered such things?

13:4 Or those eighteen, upon whom the tower in Siloam fell, and slew them, think ye that they were sinners above all men that dwelt in Jerusalem?

13:7 Why cumbereth it the ground?

13:15 Doth not each one of you on the sabbath loose his ox or his ass from the stall, and lead him away to watering?

13:16 And ought not this woman, being a daughter of Abraham, whom Satan hath bound, lo, these eighteen years, be loosed from this bond on the sabbath day?

13:18 Unto what is the kingdom of God like?

13:18 And whereunto shall I resemble it?

13:20 Whereunto shall I liken the kingdom of God?

14:3 Is it lawful to heal on the sabbath day?

14:5 Which of you shall have an ass or an ox fallen into a pit, and will not straightway pull him out on the sabbath day?

14:28 For which of you, intending to build a tower, sitteth not down first, and counteth the cost, whether he have sufficient to finish it?

14:31 What king, going to make war against another king, sitteth not down first, and consulteth whether he be able with ten thousand to meet him that cometh against him with twenty thousand?

14:34 If the salt have lost his savour, wherewith shall it be seasoned?

15:4 What man of you, having an hundred sheep, if he lose one of them, doth not leave the ninety and nine in the wilderness, and go after that which is lost, until he find it?

15:8 Either what woman having ten pieces of silver, if she lose one piece, doth not light a candle, and sweep the house, and seek diligently till she find it?

16:2 How is it that I hear this of thee?

16:3 What shall I do?

16:5 How much owest thou unto my lord?

16:7 And how much owest thou?

16:11 If therefore ye have not been faithful in the unrighteous mammon, who will commit to your trust the true riches?

16:12 And if ye have not been faithful in that which is another man's, who shall give you that which is your own?

17:7 Which of you, having a servant plowing or feeding cattle, will say unto him by and by, when he is come from the field, Go and sit down to meat?

17:8 And will not rather say unto him, Make ready wherewith I may sup, and gird thyself, and serve me, till I have eaten and drunken; and afterward thou shalt eat and drink?

17:9 Doth he thank that servant because he did the things that were commanded him?

17:17 Were there not ten cleansed?

17:17 But where are the nine?

18:7 Shall not God avenge his own elect, which cry day and night unto him, though he bear long with them?

18:8 When the Son of man cometh, shall he find faith on the earth?

18:19 Why callest thou me good?

18:41 What wilt thou that I shall do unto thee?

19:23 Wherefore then gavest not thou my money into the bank, that at my coming I might have required mine own with usury?

19:31 Why do ye loose him?

20:4 The baptism of John, was it from heaven, or of men?

20:13 What shall I do?

20:15 What therefore shall the lord of the vineyard do unto them?

20:17 What is this then that is written, The stone which the builders rejected, the same is become the head of the corner?

20:23 Why tempt ye me?

20:24 Whose image and superscription hath it?

20:41 How say they that Christ is David's son?

20:44 How is he then his son?

22:11 Where is the guest chamber, where I shall eat the passover with my disciples?

22:27 For whether is greater, he that sitteth at meat, or he that serveth?

22:27 Is not he that sitteth at meat?

22:35 When I sent you without purse, and scrip, and shoes, lacked ye any thing?

22:46 Why sleep ye?

22:48 Betrayest thou the Son of man with a kiss?

22:52 Be ye come out, as against a thief, with swords and staves?

23:31 If they do these things in a green tree, what shall be done in the dry?

24:5 Why seek ye the living among the dead?

24:17 What manner of communications are these that ye have one to another, as ye walk, and are sad?

24:19 What things?

24:26 Ought not Christ to have suffered these things, and to enter into his glory?

24:32 Did not our heart burn within us, while he talked with us by the way, and while he opened to us the scriptures?

24:38 Why are ye troubled?

24:38 And why do thoughts arise in your hearts?

24:41 Have ye here any meat?

The Gospel according to
John

1:38 What seek ye?

1:50 Because I said unto thee, I saw thee under the fig tree, believest thou?

2:4 Woman, what have I to do with thee?

3:10 Art thou a master of Israel, and knowest not these things?

3:12 If I have told you earthly things, and ye believe not, how shall ye believe, if I tell you of heavenly things?

5:6 Wilt thou be made whole?

5:44 How can ye believe, which receive honour one of another, and seek not the honour that cometh from God only?

5:47 If ye believe not his writings, how shall ye believe my words?

6:5 Whence shall we buy bread, that these may eat?

6:61 Doth this offend you?

6:62 What and if ye shall see the Son of man ascend up where he was before?

6:67 Will ye also go away?

6:70 Have not I chosen you twelve, and one of you is a devil?

7:19 Did not Moses give you the law, and yet none of you keepeth the law?

7:19 Why go ye about to kill me?

7:23 If a man on the sabbath day receive circumcision, that the law of Moses should not be broken; are ye angry at me, because I have made a man every whit whole on the sabbath day?

8:10 Woman, where are those thine accusers?

8:10 Hath no man condemned thee?

8:43 Why do ye not understand my speech?

8:46 Which of you convinceth me of sin?

8:46 And if I say the truth, why do ye not believe me?

9:35 Dost thou believe on the Son of God?

10:32 Many good works have I shewed you from my Father; for which of those works do ye stone me?

10:34 Is it not written in your law, I said, Ye are gods?

10:36 Say ye of him, whom the Father hath sanctified, and sent into the world, Thou blasphemest; because I said, I am the Son of God?

11:9 Are there not twelve hours in the day?

11:26 Whosoever liveth and believeth in me shall never die. Believest thou this?

11:34 Where have ye laid him?

11:40 Said I not unto thee, that, if thou wouldest believe, thou shouldest see the glory of God?

12:27 Now is my soul troubled; and what shall I say?

12:38 Lord, who hath believed our report?

12:38 And to whom hath the arm of the Lord been revealed?

13:12 Know ye what I have done to you?

13:38 Wilt thou lay down thy life for my sake?

14:9 Have I been so long time with you, and yet hast thou not known me, Philip?

14:9 He that hath seen me hath seen the Father; and how sayest thou then, Shew us the Father?

14:10 Believest thou not that I am in the Father, and the Father in me?

16:5 But now I go my way to him that sent me; and none of you asketh me, Whither goest thou?

16:19 Do ye enquire among yourselves of that I said, A little while, and ye shall not see me: and again, a little while, and ye shall see me?

16:31 Do ye now believe?

18:4 Whom seek ye?

18:7 Whom seek ye?

18:11 Put up thy sword into the sheath: the cup which my Father hath given me, shall I not drink it?

18:20 Why askest thou me?

18:23 If I have spoken evil, bear witness of the evil: but if well, why smitest thou me?

18:34 Sayest thou this thing of thyself, or did others tell it thee of me?

18:35 Am I a Jew?

18:35 Thine own nation and the chief priests have delivered thee unto me: what hast thou done?

18:37 Art thou a king then?

18:38 What is truth?

19:9 Whence art thou?

19:10 Speakest thou not unto me?

19:10 Knowest thou not that I have power to crucify thee, and have power to release thee?

19:15 Shall I crucify your King?

20:13 Woman, why weepest thou?

20:15 Woman, why weepest thou?

20:15 Whom seekest thou?

21:5 Children, have ye any meat?

21:15 Simon, son of Jonas, lovest thou me more than these?

21:16 Simon, son of Jonas, lovest thou me?

21:17 Simon, son of Jonas, lovest thou me?

21:22 If I will that he tarry till I come, what is that to thee? follow thou me.

21:23 Then went this saying abroad among the brethren, that that disciple should not die: yet Jesus said not unto him, He shall not die; but, If I will that he tarry till I come, what is that to thee?

Questions Asked of Jesus

The Gospel according to
Matthew

8:14 But John forbade him, saying, I have need to be baptized of thee, and comest thou to me?

8:29 What have we to do with thee, Jesus, thou Son of God?

8:29 Art thou come hither to torment us before the time?

9:14 Why do we and the Pharisees fast oft, but thy disciples fast not?

11:3 Art thou he that should come, or do we look for another?

12:10 Is it lawful to heal on the sabbath days? that they might accuse him.

13:10 Why speakest thou unto them in parables?

15:12 Knowest thou that the Pharisees were offended, after they heard this saying?

15:33 Whence should we have so much bread in the wilderness, as to fill so great a multitude?

17:19 Why could not we cast him out?

18:21 How oft shall my brother sin against me, and I forgive him?

18:21 Till seven times?

19:3 Is it lawful for a man to put away his wife for every cause?

19:7 Why did Moses then command to give a writing of divorcement, and to put her away?

19:16 Good Master, what good thing shall I do, that I may have eternal life?

19:17,18, if thou wilt enter into life, keep the commandments. He saith unto [Jesus] which?

19:25 Who then can be saved?

19:27 We have forsaken all, and followed thee; what shall we have therefore?

21:16 Hearest thou what these say?

21:23 By what authority doest thou these things?

21:23 And who gave thee this authority?

22:17 What thinkest thou?

22:17 Is it lawful to give tribute unto Caesar, or not?

22:24,25.26,27,28 Master, Moses said, if a man die, having no children, his brother shall marry his wife, and raise up seed unto his brother. Now there were with us seven brethren: and the first, when he had married a wife, deceased, and having no issue, left his wife unto his brother: likewise the second also, and the third, unto the seventh. And last of all the woman died also. Therefore in the resurrection whose wife shall she be of the seven? for they all had her

22:36 Master, which is the great commandment in the law?

24:3 When shall these things be?

24:3 And what shall be the sign of thy coming, and of the end of the world?

26:17 Where wilt thou that we prepare for thee to eat the passover?

26:22 Lord, is it I?

26:25 Master, is it I?

26:62 Answerest thou nothing?

26:62 What is it which these witness against thee?

26:68 Who is he that smote thee?

27:11 Art thou the King of the Jews?

27:13 Hearest thou not how many things they witness against thee?

The Gospel according to
Mark

1:24 What have we to do with thee, thou Jesus of Nazareth?

1:24 Art thou come to destroy us?

2:18 Why do the disciples of John and of the Pharisees fast, but thy disciples fast not?

2:24 Why do they on the sabbath day that which is not lawful?

4:38 Master, carest thou not that we perish?

5:7 What have I to do with thee, Jesus, thou Son of the most high God?

6:37 Shall we go and buy two hundred pennyworth of bread, and give them to eat?

7:5 Why walk not thy disciples according to the tradition of the elders, but eat bread with unwashen hands?

9:11 Why say the scribes that Elias must first come?

9:28 Why could not we cast him out?

10:2 Is it lawful for a man to put away his wife?

10:17 Good Master, what shall I do that I may inherit eternal life?

10:26 Who then can be saved?

11:28 By what authority doest thou these things?

11:28 And who gave thee this authority to do these things?

12:14 Is it lawful to give tribute to Caesar, or not?

12:15 Shall we give, or shall we not give?

12:20,21,22,23 Now there were seven brethren: and the first took a wife, and dying left no seed. And the second took her, and died, neither left he any seed: and the third likewise. And the seven had her, and left no seed: last of all the woman died also. In the resurrection therefore, when they shall rise, whose wife shall she be of them?

12:28 Which is the first commandment of all?

13:4 Tell us, when shall these things be?

13:4 And what shall be the sign when all these things shall be fulfilled?

14:12 Where wilt thou that we go and prepare that thou mayest eat the passover?

14:18,19 As they sat and did eat, Jesus said, Verily I say unto you, One of you which eateth with me shall betray me. And they began to be sorrowful, and to say unto him one by one, Is it I?

14:19 And another said, Is it I?

14:60 Answerest thou nothing?

14:60 What is it which these witness against thee?

14:61 Art thou the Christ, the Son of the Blessed?

15:2 Art thou the King of the Jews?

15:4 Answerest thou nothing?

The Gospel according to
Luke

2:48 Son, why hast thou thus dealt with us?

4:34 What have we to do with thee, thou Jesus of Nazareth?

4:34 Art thou come to destroy us?

5:33 Why do the disciples of John fast often, and make prayers, and likewise the disciples of the Pharisees; but thine eat and drink?

6:2 Why do ye that which is not lawful to do on the sabbath days?

7:20 Art thou he that should come?

7:20 Or look we for another?

8:9 What might this parable be?

8:28 What have I to do with thee, Jesus, thou Son of God most high?

8:45 Master, the multitude throng thee and press thee, and sayest thou, Who touched me?

9:54 Wilt thou that we command fire to come down from heaven, and consume them, even as Elias did?

10:25 Master, what shall I do to inherit eternal life?

10:29 Who is my neighbour?

10:40 Dost thou not care that my sister hath left me to serve alone?

12:41 Speakest thou this parable unto us, or even to all?

18:18 Good Master, what shall I do to inherit eternal life?

18:26 Who then can be saved?

20:2 Tell us, by what authority doest thou these things?

20:2 Or who is he that gave thee this authority?

20:22 Is it lawful for us to give tribute unto Caesar, or no?

20:28,29,30,31,32,33 Master, Moses wrote unto us, If any man's brother die, having a wife, and he die without children, that his brother should take his wife, and raise up seed unto his brother. There were therefore seven brethren: and the first took a wife, and died without children. And the second took her to wife, and he died childless. And the third took her; and in like manner the seven also: and they left no children, and died. Last of all the woman died also. Therefore in the resurrection whose wife of them is she?

21:7 When shall these things be?

21:7 And what sign will there be when these things shall come to pass?

22:9 Where wilt thou that we prepare?

22:49 Lord, shall we smite with the sword?

22:64 Prophesy, who is it that smote thee?

22:67 Art thou the Christ?

22:71 What need we any further witness?

23:3 Art thou the King of the Jews?

24:18 Art thou only a stranger in Jerusalem, and hast not known the things which are come to pass there in these days?

The Gospel according to

John

1:38 Rabbi, (which is to say, being interpreted, Master,) where dwellest thou?

1:48 Whence knowest thou me?

2:18 What sign shewest thou unto us, seeing that thou doest these things?

2:20 Forty and six years was this temple in building, and wilt thou rear it up in three days?

3:4 How can a man be born when he is old?

3:4 Can he enter the second time into his mother's womb, and be born?

3:9 How can these things be?

4:9 Then saith the woman of Samaria unto him, How is it that thou, being a Jew, askest drink of me, which am a woman of Samaria? for the Jews have no dealings with the Samaritans.

4:11 Sir, thou hast nothing to draw with, and the well is deep: from whence then hast thou that living water?

4:12 Art thou greater than our father Jacob, which gave us the well, and drank thereof himself, and his children, and his cattle?

6:9 There is a lad here, which hath five barley loaves, and two small fishes: but what are they among so many?

6:25 Rabbi, when camest thou hither?

6:28 What shall we do, that we might work the works of God?

6:30 What sign shewest thou then, that we may see, and believe thee?

6:30 What dost thou work?

6:68 Lord, to whom shall we go?

7:20 Thou hast a devil: who goeth about to kill thee?

8:5 Now Moses in the law commanded us, that such should be stoned: but what sayest thou?

8:19 Where is thy Father?

8:25 Who art thou?

8:33 We be Abraham's seed, and were never in bondage to any man: how sayest thou, Ye shall be made free?

8:48 Say we not well that thou art a Samaritan, and hast a devil?

8:53 Art thou greater than our father Abraham, which is dead?

8:53 Whom makest thou thyself?

8:57 Thou art not yet fifty years old, and hast thou seen Abraham?

9:2 Master, who did sin, this man, or his parents, that he was born blind?

9:36 Who is he, Lord, that I might believe on him?

9:40 Are we blind also?

10:24 How long dost thou make us to doubt?

11:8 Master, the Jews of late sought to stone thee; and goest thou thither again?

12:34 We have heard out of the law that Christ abideth for ever: and how sayest thou, The Son of man must be lifted up?

12:34 Who is this Son of man?

13:6 Lord, dost thou wash my feet?

13:25 Lord, who is it?

13:36 Lord, whither goest thou?

13:37 Lord, why cannot I follow thee now?

14:5 Lord, we know not whither thou goest; and how can we know the way?

14:22 Lord, how is it that thou wilt manifest thyself unto us, and not unto the world?

18:22 Answerest thou the high priest so?

18:26 Did not I see thee in the garden with him?

18:33 Art thou the King of the Jews?

18:35 Am I a Jew?

18:35 Thine own nation and the chief priests have delivered thee unto me: what hast thou done?

18:37 Art thou a king then?

18:38 What is truth?

19:9 Whence art thou?

19:10 Speakest thou not unto me?

19:10 Knowest thou not that I have power to crucify thee, and have power to release thee?

21:20 Lord, which is he that betrayeth thee?

21:21 Lord, and what shall this man do?

Questions Neither Asked
By Nor to Jesus

The Gospel according to
Matthew

2:2 Where is he that is born King of the Jews?

3:7 Who hath warned you to flee from the wrath to come?

9:11 Why eateth your Master with publicans and sinners?

12:23 Is not this the son of David?

13:27 Didst not thou sow good seed in thy field?

13:27 From whence then hath it tares?

13:28 Wilt thou then that we go and gather them up?

13:54 Whence hath this man this wisdom, and these mighty works?

13:55 Is not this the carpenter's son?

13:55 Is not his mother called Mary?

13:55 And his brethren, James, and Joses, and Simon, and Judas?

13:56 And his sisters, are they not all with us?

13:56 Whence then hath this man all these things?

18:33 Shouldest not thou also have had compassion on thy fellowservant, even as I had pity on thee?

20:6 Why stand ye here all the day idle?

20:13 I do thee no wrong: didst not thou agree with me for a penny?

20:15 Is it not lawful for me to do what I will with mine own?

20:15 Is thine eye evil, because I am good?

21:10 Who is this?

21:25 If we shall say, From heaven; he will say unto us, Why did ye not then believe him?

22:12 Friend, how camest thou in hither not having a wedding garment?

25:37 Lord, when saw we thee an hungred, and fed thee?

25:37 Or thirsty, and gave thee drink?

25:38 When saw we thee a stranger, and took thee in?

25:38 Or naked, and clothed thee?

25:39 Or when saw we thee sick, or in prison, and came unto thee?

25:44 Lord, when saw we thee an hungred, or athirst, or a stranger, or naked, or sick, or in prison, and did not minister unto thee?

26:8 To what purpose is this waste?

26:15 What will ye give me, and I will deliver him unto you?

26:65 What further need have we of witnesses?

26:66 What think ye?

27:4 What is that to us?

27:17 Whom will ye that I release unto you?

27:17 Barabbas, or Jesus which is called Christ?

27:21 Whether of the twain will ye that I release unto you?

27:22 What shall I do then with Jesus which is called Christ?

27:23 Why, what evil hath he done?

The Gospel according to
Mark

1:27 What thing is this?

1:27 What new doctrine is this?

2:7 Why doth this man thus speak blasphemies?

2:7 Who can forgive sins but God only?

2:16 How is it that he eateth and drinketh with publicans and sinners?

4:41 What manner of man is this, that even the wind and the sea obey him?

5:35 Why troublest thou the Master any further?

6:2 From whence hath this man these things?

6:2 And what wisdom is this which is given unto him, that even such mighty works are wrought by his hands?

6:3 Is not this the carpenter, the son of Mary, the brother of James, and Joses, and of Juda, and Simon?

6:3 And are not his sisters here with us?

6:24 What shall I ask?

11:5 What do ye, loosing the colt?

14:4 Why was this waste of the ointment made?

14:63 What need we any further witnesses?

14:64 What think ye?

15:9 Will ye that I release unto you the King of the Jews?

15:12 What will ye then that I shall do unto him whom ye call the King of the Jews?

15:14 Why, what evil hath he done?

16:3 Who shall roll us away the stone from the door of the sepulchre?

The Gospel according to
Luke

1:18 Whereby shall I know this?

1:34 How shall this be, seeing I know not a man?

1:43 Whence is this to me, that the mother of my Lord should come to me?

3:7 O generation of vipers, who hath warned you to flee from the wrath to come?

3:10 What shall we do then?

3:12 Master, what shall we do?

3:14 What shall we do?

4:22 Is not this Joseph's son?

5:21 Who is this which speaketh blasphemies?

5:21 Who can forgive sins, but God alone?

5:30 Why do ye eat and drink with publicans and sinners?

6:2 Why do ye that which is not lawful to do on the sabbath days?

6:3,4 Have ye not read so much as this, what David did, when himself was an hungred, and they which were with him; How he went into the house of God, and did take and eat the shewbread, and gave also to them that were with him; which it is not lawful to eat but for the priests alone?

7:19 Art thou he that should come?

7:19 Or look we for another?

7:49 Who is this that forgiveth sins also?

9:9 Who is this, of whom I hear such things?

13:7 Why cumbereth it the ground?

16:2 How is it that I hear this of thee?

16:3 What shall I do?

16:5 How much owest thou unto my lord?

16:7 And how much owest thou?

19:31 Why do ye loose him?

19:33 Why loose ye the colt?

20:5 If we shall say, From heaven; he will say, Why then believed ye him not?

23:22 Why, what evil hath he done?

23:40 Dost not thou fear God, seeing thou art in the same condemnation?

24:5 Why seek ye the living among the dead?

The Gospel according to
John

1:19 Who art thou?

1:21 What then?

1:21 Art thou Elias?

1:21 Art thou that prophet?

1:22 Who art thou?

1:22 What sayest thou of thyself?

1:25 Why baptizest thou then, if thou be not that Christ, nor Elias, neither that prophet?

1:46 Can there any good thing come out of Nazareth?

4:27 What seekest thou?

4:27 Why talkest thou with her?

4:29 Come, see a man, which told me all things that ever I did: is not this the Christ?

4:33 Hath any man brought him ought to eat?

5:12 What man is that which said unto thee, Take up thy bed, and walk?

6:42 Is not this Jesus, the son of Joseph, whose father and mother we know?

6:42 How is it then that he saith, I came down from heaven?

6:52 How can this man give us his flesh to eat?

6:60 This is an hard saying; who can hear it?

7:11 Where is he?

7:15 How knoweth this man letters, having never learned?

7:25 Is not this he, whom they seek to kill?

7:26 Do the rulers know indeed that this is the very Christ?

7:31 When Christ cometh, will he do more miracles than these which this man hath done?

7:35 Whither will he go, that we shall not find him?

7:35 Will he go unto the dispersed among the Gentiles, and teach the Gentiles?

7:36 What manner of saying is this that he said, Ye shall seek me, and shall not find me: and where I am, thither ye cannot come?

7:41 Shall Christ come out of Galilee?

7:42 Hath not the scripture said, That Christ cometh of the seed of David, and out of the town of Bethlehem, where David was?

7:45 Why have ye not brought him?

7:47 Are ye also deceived?

7:48 Have any of the rulers or of the Pharisees believed on him?

7:51 Doth our law judge any man, before it hear him, and know what he doeth?

7:52 Art thou also of Galilee?

8:22 Will he kill himself?

9:8 Is not this he that sat and begged?

9:10 How were thine eyes opened?

9:12 Where is he?

9:16 How can a man that is a sinner do such miracles?

9:17 What sayest thou of him, that he hath opened thine eyes?

9:19 Is this your son, who ye say was born blind?

9:19 How then doth he now see?

9:26 What did he to thee?

9:26 How opened he thine eyes?

9:27 I have told you already, and ye did not hear: wherefore would ye hear it again?

9:27 Will ye also be his disciples?

9:34 Thou wast altogether born in sins, and dost thou teach us?

10:20 He hath a devil, and is mad; why hear ye him?

10:21 Can a devil open the eyes of the blind?

11:37 Could not this man, which opened the eyes of the blind, have caused that even this man should not have died?

11:47 What do we? for this man doeth many miracles.

11:56 What think ye, that he will not come to the feast?

12:5 Why was not this ointment sold for three hundred pence, and given to the poor?

12:19 Perceive ye how ye prevail nothing? behold, the world is gone after him.

16:17 What is this that he saith unto us, A little while, and ye shall not see me: and again, a little while, and ye shall see me: and, Because I go to the Father?

16:18 What is this that he saith, A little while? we cannot tell what he saith.

18:17 Art not thou also one of this man's disciples?

18:25 Art not thou also one of his disciples?

18:26 Did not I see thee in the garden with him?

18:29 What accusation bring ye against this man?

18:29 Will ye therefore that I release unto you the King of the Jews?

19:15 Shall I crucify your King?

20:13 Woman, why weepest thou?

21:12 Who art thou?

Questions? Or Not!

OLD TESTAMENT

NUMBERS

14:2 And all the children of Israel murmured against Moses and against Aaron: and the whole congregation said unto them, Would God that we had died in the land of Egypt!

14:2 or would God we had died in this wilderness!

23:23 Surely there is no enchantment against Jacob, neither is there any divination against Israel: according to this time it shall be said of Jacob and of Israel, What hath God wrought!

24:5 How goodly are thy tents, O Jacob, and thy tabernacles, O Israel!

DEUTERONOMY

9:2 A people great and tall, the children of the Anakims, whom thou knowest, and of whom thou hast heard say, Who can stand before the children of Anak!

33:29 Happy art thou, O Israel: who is like unto thee, O people saved by the LORD, the shield of thy help, and who is the sword of thy excellency! and thine enemies shall be found liars unto thee; and thou shalt tread upon their high places.

JOSHUA

7:7 would to God we had been content, and dwelt on the other side Jordan!

7:8 O Lord, what shall I say, when Israel turneth their backs before their enemies!

THE SECOND BOOK OF SAMUEL

1:19 The beauty of Israel is slain upon thy high places: how are the mighty fallen!

1:25 How are the mighty fallen in the midst of the battle! O Jonathan, thou wast slain in thine high places.

1:27 How are the mighty fallen, and the weapons of war perished!

THE SECOND BOOK OF THE CHRONICLES

6:18 behold, heaven and the heaven of heavens cannot contain thee; how much less this house which I have built!

PSALM

3:1 [[A Psalm of David, when he fled from Absalom his son.]] LORD, how are they increased that trouble me! many are they that rise up against me.

71:19 Thy righteousness also, O God, is very high, who has done great things: O God, who is like unto thee!

113:5, 6 Who is like unto the LORD our God, who dwelleth on high, Who humbleth himself to behold the things that are in heaven, and in the earth

ISAIAH

1:21 How is the faithful city become an harlot! It was full of judgment; righteousness lodged in it; but now murderers.

14:12 How art thou fallen from heaven, O Lucifer, son of the morning!

14:12 how art thou cut down to the ground, which didst weaken the nations!

JEREMIAH

48:17 (How is the strong staff broken, and the beautiful rod!)

48:39 They shall howl, saying, How is it broken down!

48:39 how hath Moab turned the back with shame! so shall Moab be a derision and a dismaying to all them about him.

49:25 How is the city of praise not left, the city of my joy!

50:23 How is the hammer of the whole earth cut asunder and broken!

50:23 how is Babylon become a desolation among the nations!

51:41 How is Sheshach taken!

51:41 and how is the praise of the whole earth surprised!

51:41 how is Babylon become an astonishment among the nations!

LAMENTATIONS Of JEREMIAH

1:1 How doth the city sit solitary, that was full of people!

1:1 How is she become as a widow!

1:1 she that was great among the nations, and princess among the provinces, how is she become tributary!

2:1 How hath the Lord covered the daughter of Zion with a cloud in his anger, and cast down from heaven unto the earth the beauty of Israel, and remembered not his footstool in the day of his anger!

4:1 How is the gold become dim!

4:1 how is the most fine gold changed! The stones of the sanctuary are poured out in the top of every street.

4:2 The precious sons of Zion, comparable to fine gold, how are they esteemed as earthen pitchers, the work of the hands of the potter!

EZEKIEL

16:30, 31, 32 How weak is thine heart, saith the Lord GOD, seeing thou doest all these things, the work of an imperious whorish woman; In that thou buildest thine eminent place in the head of every way, and makest thine high place in every street; and hast not been as an harlot, in that thou scornest hire; But as a wife that committeth adultery, which taketh strangers instead of her husband!

DANIEL

4:3 How great are his signs!

4:3 and how mighty are his wonders! his kingdom is an everlasting kingdom, and his dominion is from generation to generation.

JOEL

1:18 How do the beasts groan! The herds of cattle are perplexed, because they have no pasture; yea, the flocks of sheep are made desolate.

OBADIAH

1:5 If thieves came to thee, if robbers by night, (how art thou cut off!)

1:6 How are the things of Esau searched out!

1:6 how are his hidden things sought up!

HABAKKUK

1:2 O LORD, how long shall I cry, and thou wilt not hear!

1:2 even cry out unto thee of violence, and thou wilt not save!

NEW TESTAMENT

MATTHEW

6:23 But if thine eye be evil, thy whole body shall be full of darkness. If therefore the light that is in thee be darkness, how great is that darkness!

8:27 What manner of man is this, that even the winds and the sea obey him!

21:20 How soon is the fig tree withered away!

MARK

10:23 And Jesus looked round about, and saith unto his disciples, How hardly shall they that have riches enter into the kingdom of God!

10:24 And the disciples were astonished at his words. But Jesus answereth again, and saith unto them, Children, how hard is it for them that trust in riches to enter into the kingdom of God!

LUKE

1:66 And all they that heard them laid them up in their hearts, saying, What manner of child shall this be! And the hand of the Lord was with him.

4:36 And they were all amazed, and spake among themselves, saying, What a word is this! For with authority and power he commandeth the unclean spirits, and they come out.

8:25 And they being afraid wondered, saying one to another, What manner of man is this! For he commandeth even the winds and water, and they obey him.

12:50 (I have a baptism to be baptized with; and how am I straitened till it be accomplished!)

15:17 And when he came to himself, he said, How many hired servants of my father's have bread enough and to spare, and I perish with hunger!

18:24 And when Jesus saw that he was very sorrowful, he said, How hardly shall they that have riches enter into the kingdom of God!